I Am the Christian
the Devil
Warned You About

I Am the Christian the Devil Warned You About

by **Mario Murillo**
Edited by
Carol Ann Murillo

Fresh Fire Communications
Danville, California
1996

CONTENTS

CHAPTER ONE

My Unplanned Visit to Hell

It all began one night when my bed exploded into flames and I was sucked through the floor. I found myself plunged into intense blackness and hurled downward at an astonishing rate of speed. I began to scream. My scream was not human. It came tearing its way out of my soul. This scream should have burst my lungs and ruined my throat. Instead my voice kept getting louder and louder.

Thoughts were crashing against my skull. My mind could not process what was happening. Imagine the darkest darkness you have ever known. I promise you that this blackness would make it seem as noonday. How could my soul be damned since I was a Christian? This question ignited fright so intense I felt in my soul that I was dead, since no one could live through such fear.

I was tumbling and falling, and just when I

thought I had seen the worst, I caught a glimpse of a mass below me. I could not make it out, but it was ugly and it undulated. As I raced toward whatever it was, I was still screaming ever more loudly.

All at once I heard voices more mournful and pitiful and painful and hideous than my own. So much so that their wailing, though not as loud as my screaming, brought me a more unbearable sensation. As I grew nearer to the sound my scream changed and began to more closely resemble the macabre gushings of those below me. I had joined the chorus of the damned.

Suddenly I crashed into the mass with such force that it should have pulverized my bones. The substance was liquid and I flailed my arms desperately trying to find the surface. It was an ocean, and its substance was an emulsion of all that was lost and forsaken. Each splash left a residue on my face and arms that was repugnant and indelible. My body wilted; my wails were now automatic. I was resigned to my doom.

An evil current carried me toward a flaming coast that I saw far off in the distance. I knew that on that shore I would find my eternal punishment.

At last I reached the coastline and pulled myself from the malevolent mire. Demons appeared. By all rights, their malignant visages should have horrified me, but by now I had seen so much that they were just a mild addition to my already existing torment. The demons did not try to torture me, but in fact, they ignored me. Or was it that they could not see me?

No one can muffle their wailing in Hell so at least they should have heard me, but they seemed not to hear me. Were they overlooking me because some further fate even more gruesome awaited me?

I trudged through Hell instinctively knowing what direction I should take. I heard the other voices of the damned. In fact, we could hear each others' wails but we could not communicate.

The weight of my eternal judgment had now crushed my spirit and slowed my pace down to a mere shuffle. I headed toward a place worse than I had seen thus far. I knew it and yet I could not stop moving forward.

After I had moved for what seemed miles, my mouth was parched but I knew I would not be given the mercy of dying of thirst. My exhausted legs wobbled, and my body was limp. I knew that I would never again know the blessing of sleep nor could I stop moving no matter how weak I became.

At that moment, a flock of demons sailed past me. Their revolting leathery wings beat furiously. They darted past me again as if I were invisible.

Then the strangest thing happened. My mind, churning with thoughts of my unspeakable fate, found room for other ideas. How was it, for example, that I could know that these minions of Satan were his elite force or that they could fly because Lucifer had given them wings as rewards for great exploits? Why would I even be thinking of this in the midst of my torment? Even more intriguing was my conviction that they were headed for a summit with Satan and that all of Hell was vibrating with excitement over this gathering.

For the first time since I had laid in my own bed, my torment leveled off. My body, still weak, quickened its pace, but now it was by my own choosing. My wails subsided and I began to feel a measure of strength. My scant Bible knowledge mingled with a new awareness in my mind. I whispered quietly, "Maybe there is still hope."

Another realization emerged within me. This could not be the final Hell of the Bible. Hades is not a place where demons manage lost souls or conduct meetings. The final fire is a lake where Satan is cast first, then his hosts, and then human souls that rejected Christ on Earth.

I was compelled to get to this meeting of devils but I did not know why. My heart and my conscience still smote me with shame. "Even if this was not yet Hell," I said, convulsing, "then what must Hell be like and what reason did I have for thinking that I was not yet marked for damnation?"

I did not know how I understood all these things. I could not tell why this hideous gathering seemed to hold some hope for me. I did not fear anything about my evil surroundings; I cared only about getting to the meeting. Each step strengthened my body and resolve until I was actually running toward it.

My mind slowly filled with more understanding. I was truly invisible to these horrible beings. This was the realm of Satan. This place was where he had his throne.

Lucifer is so vicious that he fills his caverns with the cries of Man's misery. He collects the sounds of war, grief, and horror and pipes them in as background music. This is the sound that I mistook for the chorus of the damned.

All of these thoughts filled my mind as I pressed my way toward the great event. I followed the road to its summit and found myself standing on the rim of a great crater. Far below me, spread out in all its evil glory, was Lucifer's central command. My only access was a steep and treacherous stairway that led down to the bottom of the crater. I had no hesitation, no sense of danger, nor did those foreboding stairs scare me, for it was nothing compared to the horror I had survived already. I began my descent. I thought that perhaps the worst was over, but I could not have been more mistaken.

CHAPTER TWO

I Meet Satan

It was an eternity to the bottom of those stone steps. At last I reached the entrance to the gathering of devils. The meeting was being held in a dreadful amphitheater. As I drew closer, I could finally make out the irritating sounds that had been damaging my ears all the way down the stairway.

Demons were flying in mass profusion about the throne of Satan. They resembled a swarm of giant locusts. This was an aerial tribute to the Devil.

Having had so many extreme emotions awakened in me during this night, you would think by now I would be ready for anything. But out of my spirit rose a shocking holy rage at the blasphemy of these beings. I became a single, imploring soul before God that he would pour out His wrath there and then at these proceedings. But this rage cooled and gave way to a sense of higher purpose.

As I looked around, Satan was not visible to me, except in flashes between the beating wings of these flying demons. Finally, Lucifer raised his arms and called the meeting to order.

Somehow I knew I should not look at Satan, so instead I fixed my gaze at his throne. It seemed alive. It writhed. It was covered with symbols of wickedness. I could see faces, as if they were in some liquid, surfacing and sinking into his throne. These were images of pure misery.

Prominently displayed upon this massive seat were the records of every war in a vivid recollection of the evolving art of mass murder Satan had taught to humankind. You could feel the grief and horror and massive bloodshed that each image recalled. There was a choice place that remembered the Jewish holocaust and a deliberately larger open space that was reserved for something even more horrendous yet to come.

The substance of Satan's throne was something infected. I could see insects unknown to Earth crawling about this thing: it was more than a throne; it was a malignant monument.

By chance I looked upon Satan's face. One glimpse and all my forgotten terror returned. I began to scream anew. A feeling that began as fear worked its way into a sense of such total despair that I collapsed in pain. I doubled over, grabbing my stomach, and begging God to take my life. Oh, how I wished I had never been born!

Even now, I would hope that my eyes had never been cursed with that vision or that my mind had never been poisoned with such a memory. It was difficult to believe that this unholy countenance was once the Angel of Light. This was no face. It was like a collapsed star, a black hole of such gravity that it would not let light escape. But with Satan, it was everything decent, sane, and alive vacuumed out of you.

My prayers and my weeping were not answered with the relief of death but with a gentle beam of love. It changed me so that I could look again, bear the sight before me, and finish my work.

Now Lucifer beckoned the demons to hear his vile speech. Satan's voice, which would suffocate a human, infused life into these demons. I mustered all the will I had to stand and take note of the wicked plot that I was about to hear.

Now I was fully confident that I was not a damned soul, but a spy from God.

"This is it!" roared the Devil. "I am now going to reveal my master stroke against mankind, an attack that I have waited to release which will be remembered as a wonder of all the ages. I am prepared to defeat the Unseen Hand that has restrained my past assaults. Behold!"

What happened next is hard to describe. A

screen, or rather a membrane, descended and floated hideously above us. On this translucent skin appeared images that graphically portrayed *the master plan*. It was a drenching of evil, a crushing, piercing flood of every wile of Beelzebub that had ever been inflicted on man. In was a confluence of disaster and deception where every decent thing would be destroyed in a global boiling cauldron of misery. The goal was clear: *harvest more souls for Hell in one campaign than the combined number of all who were damned in history*.

My teeth ground in bitter rage! My soul wailed, filled with remorse for my lukewarm Christian life. Each image before me stoked an inner volcano, the lava of which took away the wimp and left a warrior. Tears and roars alternately poured from me until there was nothing left of the man I once was. How, you may ask, did I know I was so utterly transformed? It was because I could now stare directly into the eyes of Lucifer with no ill effect and without flinching.

Now I knew that God could ask me to do anything to stop this evil plot and that I would obey without question. I carefully began to listen to detail after detail of what the Enemy had planned to do. The Devil meant to pit nation against nation in a bloodletting world war that would turn oceans red. He would snuff out the very light of decency and wipe out the witness of the Church.

Satan's vile presentation climaxed with a clear and convincing portrayal of the world's destruction. The demons could bear no more and all at once exploded into an orgy of exaltation of their dark master. The plan seemed foolproof and the toll would be astronomical. I felt helpless to do anything and my roars of rebuke fell unheard by my adversaries.

I covered my ears to deaden the hideous sounds of these cursed beings. It was no use. Their chorus became a deafening cacophony of massive train crashes and frenzied insects. The clamor was painful but I refused to stop staring at my Enemy. It seemed logical that Satan would be pleased with this plan and with the excitement of his minions, but he did not join in the celebration.

What was this strange change of expression on his face? What was this? A look of consternation? Was the Devil disconsolate?

By now I had learned to obey that inner impulse that instructed me. I was now aware that no amount of gloating by Lucifer's associates could drown out the memory of how each and every one of his past schemes, regardless of how grand their design, had in fact been hurled back at him with more than equal measure. He was sensing that his time was short. He was trying to deny the omens that reminded him of his destiny—to suffer history's most humiliating and complete judgment and execution. He was no mighty potentate on the eve of some great triumph. He was a trapped animal piecing together one last frenzied and frustrated attempt to take down as many with him as possible.

As Satan's dread increased, my boldness grew. Presently, he turned to his demons and yelled for silence. The obnoxious squeals fell into dead calm. He stared piercingly at his crack troops feeling the threat to his plan and future. He lashed out at them. "Do you fools truly believe that our strategy is fail safe? Do you think that our enemy is helpless?" I could see that these leathery creatures were genuinely bewildered by their master's statements.

"There is the threat," he continued, "that even one may yet be created." The legions of Hell gasped in recognition.

"One what?" I wondered. I was curious that every demon there knew what Satan meant and puzzled that I did not.

"Here is my pain. Here is my torture!" Satan bellowed in a shockingly uncharacteristic show of fear. This awakened no little disturbance among the demons who, one by one, tried to encourage Beelzebub. This only fueled his anger.

"One true, one fitted for war, could arise from the most unpromising situations and unleash havoc on us," Satan blurted. "This effect could grow at the speed of light until we are all driven back."

Now my heart beat with excitement and wonder. "One true what?" I murmured.

Then Satan retorted, "It is not fair that I have not been allowed to destroy the writing of the twelve secrets." I could not bear the curiosity and anticipation. *The twelve secrets?* What were they? And why were they such a fearful and threatening thing to Satan?

One certainty pervaded me. I had just heard the first of why I was in the Devil's lair.

CHAPTER THREE

I Am the Christian
the Devil Warned You About

How can I describe to you the strange sense of destiny I felt? To know that I was standing before the elite of Hell, hearing their plans, sensing their fears, and yet be totally hidden from their view? I listened with intense anticipation to what Satan would admit next.

"One authentic Christian," he wailed, "in which Christ works without resistance is all that it would take to disrupt everything." The Father of Lies contorted as if he was having a momentary seizure. His minions reeled for they had never heard him concede to saying the name of the Lord.

Lucifer continued, "One true Christian, rightly fitted for war, will be the ruin of us. And few things would aid this more than what is written in *The Twelve*.

Then a demon said, "But, Your Majesty, the writing has been stopped."

"You fool!" Satan shot back, as he flung the pathetic being clear across the crater. "It is not the writing of *The Twelve* that brings me dread. We already have an infinitely more dangerous writing, and it is everywhere—The Bible!" When he mentioned the scriptures it induced another seizure. "The danger, my misinformed warrior," said Satan, "is the meaning of *The Twelve* and the horrible way in which they show exactly what is wrong, why our enemy's followers do not obey. It awakens a keen insight into their holy book. These *Twelve* expose the exact points on which we have so effectively divided them. It tells them how to arm the places of their vulnerability. Listen, you banal beasts, if just one could read and discover how to ask and then receive, if just one would embrace their potential . . . but most of all if just one were to discover the One who is ever with them to make them strong, wise, and miraculous, then . . ." At the mention of God's Spirit, the entire company involuntarily dropped and ducked for cover.

"But Master," braved another evil spirit, "you have rid the Earth of the author of *The Twelve*, have you not?"

"Yes, but his writings still live, and I live in constant threat that someone will find them," answered Lucifer.

"But why don't we simply find the thesis and destroy it?" This apparently was a particularly stupid and enraging query that caused the Devil to grab this hapless demon by the throat and hold him aloft.

"Because, you idiot!" Satan said as he dangled the demon, "there is a sentinel, an angel, that has remained outside the author's home to this very moment guarding the document." Then he flung the leathery critter with such force that he rolled and bounced almost all the way up the same stairs I had just descended.

Next Satan recounted the story of Martin, the author of *The Twelve*. He painted a picture of a man who had been a mighty leader of the gospel in China. With intense animosity, Satan described the awesome effectiveness of this simple man. He had blasted revivals of righteousness into village after village in the remotest parts of China and won entire regions to Christ. He told how this missionary had an amazing gift of creating leaders who would carry fire to even more places. This unique expression of awakening alarmed Satan, who had seen nothing like it before and knew that it represented a model for the entire Church.

It became Satan's ambition to stop Martin. The Enemy understood that he could not assault this dedicated vessel of God from without, for that would have strengthened the resolve of his co-workers. Instead he used his religious demons to infiltrate and divide. Satan called upon his tried and true tools for halting the church: jealousy and politics, and the mismanagement tendencies of church hierarchy. But it was when Martin set to paper *The Twelve* keys to his breakthroughs in China, that Lucifer stepped up his assault against him.

Criticism from Martin's American missions board broke his heart. Powerless representatives were sent to police his activities. They returned with false reports.

The stress of seeing her husband so unfairly treated broke his wife's health and she died. He reluctantly agreed, several years later, to return home with his two sons and young daughter. His sons refused to return home. His sons refused to return home with the family, so he and his daughter left to come back to America alone. There Martin was attached to his denomination's college to teach future ministers.

Martin finished his writing of *The Twelve* in America and prepared to teach it as a college-level course. Before he could do so, Satan arose in great wrath and provoked Martin's superiors, who had never even tried to study his thesis, to brand him an extremist. The hypocrisy of their own lives is what was truly at risk. Satan used their fear of being exposed to cause them to exert pressure on Martin to renounce a document they knew nothing about.

As I stood there listening to Satan's story, my heart grieved for and bonded with this missionary. He was so loyal that he agreed to all the unreasonable demands of his leadership. His sons remained on the front lines of the mission field, but soon they too passed away from the exhaustion of their great work. Martin was left with a little cottage and a young daughter to raise. He taught for a few years, but soon the loss of his loved ones and the grief of having his life's work rejected took its toll, and he also died.

While Satan angrily rehashed all of these facts, I saw visions of what Martin looked like. As Satan ended his diatribe against this holy man, one more scene was vividly portrayed before me. It was of a more hopeful and relieved man.

Rather than destroy his treatise, Martin decided to place it in a strongbox for safekeeping. He went to the corner of his basement, removed some floorboards, and lovingly placed the metal box under the floor. He had a God-given hope that one day it would be found. The fact that Satan could not get to the box gave him the greatest agony.

The self-pitying wranglings of Lucifer now ended. An uneasy silence fell upon these gates of Hell. Watching Belial slump in his chair, I sensed that possibly this world-wide attack could be called off.

Whatever hope of this I nursed was soon dashed by the appearance of yet one more fallen angel. This time it was truly an insidious and cunning being. The demons made way for this spirit as it made its grand entrance. The fiend that approached Satan was none other than the Devil of Discouragement. He had shipwrecked more vessels of God in history than any other. He could breathe upon a man's soul and kill a vision like a frost upon tender vegetation. He was always sent in as the final option to those who troubled the Prince of Darkness most.

What a grotesque ghoul! He bowed in deference to his king and waived his freakish hand for all to listen to him.

"Lord, Mephistopheles," he began, "I am your obedient slave. I fear that you have entertained too bleak of an assessment of your situation. You are the Monarch of the Earth. Your achievements speak for themselves. Will your master plan prevail? Of course it will! It is the supreme invention, born of your eternal wisdom. It is your destiny, that for which you have existed for all time."

He proceeded to project new images upon that grisly floating screen. The triumph of Lucifer, appearing from the moment he purloined Adam's rights over the Earth, to victories of every sort, here was a nefarious demon putting on the show of his career. His viperous words infused life into the Lord of Vermin. Satan's atrocities were blazed before us. My sick soul reeled in vexation.

The fiendish frenzy continued. The demon elite rose in wave after wave of roaring praises as diabolical schemes and exploits were celebrated.

Presently, this Demon of Discouragement turned to address the core fear of Beelzebub. "Your Omnipotence, let me ask, do you really believe that the dreaded one will be created? You know what buffoons these mortals are. Even if the twelve secrets were found, the mediocres will never permit their comfortable lifestyles to be disturbed by their content. How many times has our Enemy's Spirit energized one of them to speak warnings, only to have his fire doused by their love of the world which we feed to them? Do you suppose that I would permit the writings of *The Twelve* to actually take hold? If one even attempts to pursue the document, will I not step in to wither his will? Will I not dredge up his past and prove that they are ineligible to ever be a vessel of honor? Or, I could gently whisper the impossibility of his task in such imperceptible doses that he will not notice that he has been numbed with doubt?"

Amid his dissertation, Satan was ignited with courage. His countenance regained its ignoble luster. He roared his approval.

The demon continued with abominable words cascading from his mouth. He turned into an obnoxious cheerleader who began to deride the faith of all believers in general. His voice made me seethe, and his accusations incited me as nothing had before. He had mocked and ridiculed everything holy. This began to build up a firestorm within me.

"Remember, Master," he drooled, "how much we enjoy toying with these wretched creatures who try to bring revival. When one of them gets a grip on a neglected truth, we wound them until their message is full of rancor and hurt and stripped of its potency. When a secular idea pervades a generation, we get preachers to concoct a Christian version of it and inject it into their gospel so that its power to transform is neutralized. When they get excited and are dangerously close to a massive breakthrough, we merely step behind it and push their excitement into emotional extremes. That way they are discredited by their fellow believers. But above all, you must recall how they do us proud when we teach them how to mask their cruelty under the pretense of zeal for truth. Hence, they shoot their own wounded and show no mercy."

I could listen no more. I was consumed by wrath and fury. I called out in prayer pleading to my God. Why should I be tortured by these abominations if I had no power to avenge my Lord? That inward impression that aided me so much, once more counseled me. I knew that I was to wait for a moment yet to come. I was not to waste my raging, but allow it instead, to become concentrated. I would look for the perfectly timed, divine moment.

The Demon of Discouragement's words grew even more monstrous as he boasted that Satan's final attack would not only ruin Earth, but Heaven as well. He stated that the Holy One would be dethroned and that Lucifer would own the glory.

The volcano within me rumbled anew. Something astonishing was rising in my soul. A deep and thunderous roar came out of my mouth that was louder than a million combined thunderclaps. Now the Devil could see me and hear me! The whole company was blown away like leaves in a hurricane. Satan was smashed against his throne by the roar. The mocking Demon of Discouragement was flattened against a pillar.

Now I was permitted to respond to this blasphemer. I walked right up to him and roared again, "You have counted out the believers. You have dismissed the Church's power. Let me ask you, you cursed devil bound for damnation, do you know me? Do you know who I am? Do you really think that no one will find *The Twelve* and that no one in all the Church will become one of those you dread? Think again. Do you know who I really am? I slowly put my face near his and pointed in the direction of Satan and said, "I am the Christian the Devil warned you about!"

CHAPTER FOUR

The Twelve Are Found

I woke up to find myself lying on grass. I was in a park in the middle of my own town, fully dressed in the clothes I had worn to church the night before. Anyone who may have seen me might have assumed that I had been taking a mid-morning nap. How could they know that I had just been translated from Lucifer's region?

My greatest challenge now was to restrain the supernatural still at work within me. I had believed that I was damned. Now I knew that I was redeemed!

I had seen evil in its fullness and my rage and disgust still burned within me. Because I had learned my purpose, unquenchable zeal possessed me. Compromise was unimaginable and the thought of ever returning to the bland faith that once held me was unbearable.

I had to be careful. I had to contain my emotions. It would be easy to terrify someone with a face that went from unbridled joy, to intense remorse, to unspeakable holy rage.

How can I describe to you the thrill I now felt when I looked across the street from the park and saw Martin's house?

My mind raced with questions and possibilities. Was Martin's surviving daughter still living there? She would have to be about thirty years old. Even if she was still there, how in the world could I get her to believe what I had just been through? What if she rejected everything I was about to tell her?

I got up and started for the house. I knew I had no choice. My future was all wrapped up in this encounter. My heart was beating wildly as I rapped on the door.

She was there! She was walking towards the door. She opened it, but only part way.

"Can I help you?" she asked.

I started to talk, but it was all running together. Three times I tried to begin at the beginning. I could tell that something in my eyes frightened her. She began to politely excuse herself and slowly close the door.

It was my last chance. "Please, Miranda," I said, not even realizing that I knew her name. "Your father wrote something very important and you must let his work live on."

She was still fearful, but this statement touched her, so she was willing to leave the door open slightly.

There is no way to break this kind of story tactfully, so I began to relate details that no one but she and her father could have known. She listened. I could see that she had mixed emotions. Was this a true miracle or some kind of elaborate, cruel joke?

She listened as long as she could and finally stopped me. With a look that was stern but gentle, she said, "I don't know who you are but I have learned to hate the memory of the thesis you are describing. If I let you in my house, I risk opening some very deep wounds."

I assured her that I was in earnest. By all rights, she should have sent me away, but the facts I related to her were startling enough to make her wonder. I could see that she still deeply loved and respected her father.

She slipped the chain off the door and allowed me to enter. "My father," she said to me, "was, as you said, a humble yet powerful missionary. I grew to resent the way it seemed he had thrown his life away because of his loyalty. He was a genius, a man with such clear purpose, honesty, and love, that people around him seemed to grow powerful by just being associated with him. It makes me so angry to think that his simple genius went unregarded and misunderstood by those who should have appreciated it the most."

"Upon my life," I said, "I assure you that my story is true. I know that the only way I can prove this to you is by finding your father's writings."

She interrupted me, "But he destroyed everything, even his research."

"Listen, Miranda. Your father did not die regretting his thesis. He hoped that one day it would be found and, in fact, experienced a personal victory near the end of his life that you cannot even imagine."

"How do you know this?" she implored. Then and there I opened my heart and let her hear *everything* that had transpired from my fall into the Devil's lair until the moment we were now meeting.

At last I said, "Miranda, you are not going to reopen old wounds. Your wounds are going to be healed." Still, her turmoil was great. Her inner war was overwhelming.

"How can you expect anyone to believe what you have said?" She was then silent for a long time. Slowly her expression changed and she said softly, "Somehow I believe you because of the look you have in your eyes. Few, if any, have that look. You only get it after a true bout with the Evil One, and after you face your own flesh and win a warrior's heart from God. I know that look. I saw that look in my father's eyes.

"My dad did things that no one else could even imagine. No one else had such an awesome effect on the powers of darkness.

"Let me tell you about the problem we faced in China. We were reaching a lower class of villagers. Our missions board wanted us to reach a 'higher' caste which looked down upon the people we were winning to God. We begged for more missionaries to be sent because tens of thousands were being converted at one time. None came. Our amazing results were kept muted back home by the jealous leaders.

"Finally my father began making leaders of those he had won to the Lord. He had a gift for imparting truth. They became lions of God under his tutelage. This made our mission explode even more. We all had to work to bring in the immense harvest of lives. This is what caused my mother to collapse and finally die." At this point, Miranda stopped talking, for she could no longer choke back her tears. I began to cry also. After awhile she was able to continue.

"In my father's profound grief, he buried himself in isolated prayer. We thought he was seeking consolation. He was gone for forty days, and we don't know that he even ate during his time away. When he returned, he had aged ten years and looked as if all the forces of Hell had focused themselves upon him. Later on, we found out that he began his season of prayer by warring with God to raise my mother from the dead. God would not give her back. Instead, he used my father's grief as a finishing tool. That is when the series of truths, *The Twelve*, were born. My father waged a noble battle against Satan and finally emerged with a clear understanding of these principles. He determined that they would be a living memorial to the wonderful and godly woman that was his wife.

"When the reassignment to teach came, my older brothers convinced him that it was best Dad and I return to America. They remained behind to carry on the mission. I knew it would be a difficult move, but my father's loyalty left him no choice.

"The day we left China, I knew I would ultimately be left alone. As I was saying goodbye to my older brothers, my heart told me that I would never see them again. And, of course, they did work themselves into an early grave. My father, I knew, would die as well if he was far away from his beloved China mission."

Miranda paused briefly. "When we got home," she went on to say, "my father began piecing *The Twelve* together. He was aflame each time he entered prayer. He went to prayer as one going after light and could not return alive without it. One day, I caught a glimpse of his writings, but what I read was simple and obvious. I could never understand how anyone could say that what my father wrote was not the truth.

"When he announced that he would teach *The Twelve* as a class in the college, all sorts of havoc began. Leaders who didn't know what they were talking about, who had only read bits and pieces of the work that had leaked out, attacked it. First, they went after my father's academic knowledge, then his integrity. Finally, they branded the writings as heresy. They acted so bizarre that I am sure now that you are right. Satan himself must have conspired to wipe out my father's work.

"I saw good friends of our family suddenly change. I heard the petty arguments against my father. He withdrew from teaching *The Twelve*. He was so overwrought with grief, he decided to destroy all that he had written. His heart was broken, for what turned out to be, the last time. Though he continued to teach for a little while, I knew that we were losing him." She paused here and again wept openly.

"One day, while standing before a classroom of students, making one last plea for the real and genuine Christian, my father died. That is why I came to hate his thesis. It killed him."

I said nothing, but held Miranda's hand while rivers of tears flowed. What disgust and fear fell upon me when I realized that Satan was willing to ply all of the forces of evil against this man, but never had to use anyone outside the Church to take this man out.

I had to proceed with caution and yet be bold. "Miranda, your father's writing did not kill him. These writings gave him life," I said.

"I must ask you now if we can go to the basement of your house where your father used to pray." The question startled her, but she did not bother to ask me how I knew that this was where he prayed.

After a few minutes passed, she led me downstairs to the basement. Though I had never been in this house before, each step downward seemed familiar because of what I had seen in the Devil's region.

Upon reaching the bottom of the staircase, I pointed to a door to a small storage area. "That is where he prayed."

"Yes," she said. "My family could never understand why, with all the other places where he could choose to pray, he chose that dark and dank corner."

"Well, under the floorboards of that room is the box that contains your father's thesis," I responded. Miranda's eyes widened.

All at once she stopped. "You must forgive my hesitancy," she said, "but I feel that we are about to do something that will alter both our lives forever. I want you to understand that if we do find my father's thesis in there, and you are who you say you are, and your story is true and correct, then even you, with all your experiences still may not truly understand the power and simplicity of those things for which my father lived."

At that moment I recognized that there was no holier ground on Earth. I felt as though we were both invading a shrine. This was one of the most hotly contested pieces of real estate on Earth. We were at a flashpoint of good and evil.

She asked me again, "Are you willing to pay the price that will be asked of you if you read and understand this work?"

"I have seen damnation," I told her. "More than that, I have seen the most vile master plan to destroy mankind ever conceived. You cannot come back from that without abandoning all human inhibition and fear. All that matters to me now is to find what your father has written and completely absorb it. I am not going to back down."

We took tools from nearby and together we entered the storage room and began pulling up the floorboards. There was the metal box! We eagerly, yet fearfully, opened it. There within the box, just as we had known in our hearts it would be, was a large book, a prayer diary, wrapped carefully with paper.

On the outside of the diary was an envelope. Printed on it was a note that said, "Please read this first." With quivering hands, I opened the letter. Miranda took my hand in an effort to calm me. I opened the letter and began to read its contents.

Dear Friend,

You have found this because God wanted You to find it. What you are about to read contains great and mighty truths that I am undeserving to have understood. I hope that you will feel the same humility about hearing them in your soul. It is an undeniable and unalterable fact that the Bible, the Holy Spirit, and the Lord Jesus Christ Himself, revealed twelve elements, principles, that when they are permitted to work in concert have in all times catalyzed a massive depletion of evil.

What awaits you now is the power that has turned darkness back throughout history. Please understand that once you know and grasp their essence, you must not neglect to implement them, for to do so would be the highest form of treason a child of God can commit.

Your brother, Martin

I unwrapped the book, and there I found another envelope that simply said, "To Miranda, With All My Love."

Miranda trembled as I handed her the letter from her father. What the letter said, I cannot tell, but I do know that as she read, a good cry started. These were healing words of love that only a godly father can impart to his daughter.

She excused herself and went back upstairs. I

could hear her above me praying, rejoicing, crying, and laughing as she paced back and forth reading those tender life-giving words over and over.

As for me, I took the tools and repaired the prayer room. I wanted to begin my new life in prayer right where Martin had left off with his.

Kneeling before my God as a child about to be weaned, I opened the diary and found the page that said *Secret #1.*

The Why

The One Who Knows
What Will Always
Be the Servant of
the One Who Knows *Why*

Dear Warrior,

Satan does not know why he does what he does. If he did, he would implode with despair. But if you knew why you do what you do, it would be the complete making of you.

Lucifer has merely been allowed to exist. He is deceived by design and obligated to have all of his acts ultimately recoil back on to him.

How can I prove this to you? Simply ask yourself, what single event of all time has been most devastating to the Prince of Darkness? It is the resurrection of Christ, of course! This univer-sal detonation of glory which saved man and brought unspeakable gifts of grace and righ-teousness would not have been possible without a death first.

Beelzebub committed a massive blunder in killing the Christ. Yet, he had access to all the Old Testament prophecies. He even eaves-dropped on Jesus as He taught His disciples about His death, burial, and Easter miracle. None of this helped the Devil restrain his disas-trous impulses.

There, my friend, is your edge over the enemy. He continues to make key mistakes. The Christian warrior with the *why*, will not only spot those errors, but will literally shape them into a divine counterattack.

Look at a simple example of a skilled soldier at work. The Apostle Paul wrote this about his arrest and imprisonment: "But I want you to know, brethren, that the things which happened to me have actually turned out for the further-ance of the gospel, so that it has become evident to the whole palace guard, and to all the rest, that my chains are in Christ; and most of the brethren in the Lord, having become confident by my chains, are much more bold to speak the word without fear. Some indeed preach Christ even from envy and strife, and some also from goodwill. The former preach Christ from selfish

ambition, not sincerely, supposing to add afflic-
tion to my chains . . ." [Philippians 1:12-14].

Satan meant to demoralize Paul, but Paul
seized the intention and found joy in turning a
prison cell into a gospel distribution center.

The Devil leaps from one delirious attack to
another "seeking whom he may devour." He is
helpless to heed the signs of a trap. He does not
consider what has happened before nor what
will happen again as a consequence of his
aggressions.

You, however, are capable of embracing the
driving force of the entire creation. You can act
beyond what something looks like and catch
what it means.

The word *why* packs a universe of power into
a syllable. *Why* means you own the essence, the
meaning, the purpose, and intention, and are
able to judge what you observe against the *why*.

"*What*" is defined as "that which, a thing, an
event, circumstance, or situation." Again *why*
is defined as "the intention, meaning, essence,
purpose, reason, and design."

When all she had was a *what*, Esther was
simply a primping debutante in a palace pent-
house. When she discovered *why* she had all that
she had, she bolted from her comfort zone and
went forth to save a whole race.

Nebuchadnezzar knew *what* he had dreamed,
but that was all. He was filled with anxiety and

anger. Under the threat of death, the wise men of Babylon were ordered to tell his dream and interpret it. "This," they complained, "only God can do." Daniel was brought in. The king cast him a menacing look. The tables turned and Daniel gave forth the meaning of the nightmare. Then the despot fell and paid homage to Daniel.

Then there was Saul of Tarsus, raging his way to Damascus. Without warning, he and his troupe were flattened by a God-sent laser light. All of them saw the light, but only Saul heard the Voice. Today we do not know the names of any of those that were with Saul, because all they had to describe was the light, or what they saw. But Saul heard The Voice in the light. This changed him into Paul the Apostle and infused him with a *why* that is still transforming the entire world.

Now I must talk to you about war because we *are* at war. We have been deluded into believing that there are two kinds of war, physical and spiritual, but there is only war.

War turns physical when there is a defeat in the spiritual struggle, but it is all the same war. All war, according to James, comes from our members. "Where do wars come from among you? Do they not come from your desires for pleasure that war in your members?" [James 4:1]

Lucifer has bewitched Christians into accepting a subtle lie that has huge consequences. We say the Christian life is *like a war*. It sounds innocent, but it casts a disastrous symbolism to something that is desperately real. If we are in *something like* a war, then the Bible becomes *something like* the Word of God, and we face *something like* an attack, and we put on *something like* the armor of God.

If there is a basic rule about war, it is that if you are in one, you should know it! And, my friend, you are in one.

Here comes the word *why* again. Why are you under attack? Why you should you learn to fight? Until you face the fact that you are locked in mortal combat, you will never stop being confused and you will never take adequate measures to arm yourself. Some even coddle the notion that if they remain a commonplace Christian, Satan will not attack them. But the warrior understands that the unarmed are taken out first.

In China, I read the works of a general named Sun Tzu. Though he wrote about war 2300 years ago, his wisdom is revered by the modern military establishment. I mention him because, though he speaks from worldly wisdom, he captures an insight to war that we need. His key observations will appear throughout *The Twelve*.

Sun Tzu taught a series that the experts of war

have come to recognize as the fundamental principles of war. It is believed, with great conviction, that when these factors are obeyed, they tend toward victory. When they are ignored, they guarantee defeat.

Sun Tzu taught that the primary condition that must be present before declaring war is that an army must know the exact reasons for the war, must believe in the integrity of their leadership, must have a precise, detailed goal as well as a plan that spells out the means by which victory will be sought.

He called this *the moral influence*. By "moral influence," he said, "I mean that which causes the people to be in harmony with their leaders so that they will accompany them in life and unto death without fear of mortal peril."[1]

The *moral influence* is the *why* of war. Let us examine carefully the elements that must be present before an army goes to war:

1. The war must be declared by leaders that the people trust, and the war must be declared upon a universally recognized evil.
2. Clear estimates must be made of the enemy's size and of the cost of waging war against them. These estimates must be made by experts that are deemed dependable, and provisions must be adequate.

3. A plan must be drawn up that combines: (a) the proven experience of past victories, (b) the elements of the most advanced weapons, (c) a clear intelligence concerning the enemy's location and size, (d) the fighting characteristics of the enemy, and (e) a detailed list of provisions needed to wage war.

4. Each soldier must possess a clear view, not only of the overall objective, but of their individual assignment in achieving the objective.

Sun Tsu said, "With many calculations, one can win; with few one cannot. How much less chance of victory has one who makes none at all! By this means I examine the situation and the outcome will be clearly apparent."[2]

These four elements not only make up the *why* of war, they also are the *why* of your warfare in Christ.

In Luke 14:31, Jesus said, "Or what king, going to make war against another king, does not sit down first and consider whether he is able with ten thousand to meet him who comes against him with twenty thousand?"

These four factors are what we must focus on as Christian warriors:

1. *War has been declared on an undeniable*

evil. We know why Jesus declared war on Satan. He made His intention clear. "For this purpose the Son of God was manifested, that He might destroy the works of the devil" [I John 3:8].

We know that He is righteous and has proven His trust by not only dying on the cross, but by winning the first attack Himself. ". . . having wiped out the handwriting of requirements that was against us, which was contrary to us. And He has taken it out of the way, having nailed it to the cross. Having disarmed principalities and powers, He made a public spectacle of them, triumphing over them in it" [Colossians 2:14-15].

2. *We know that the Holy Spirit gives us accurate estimates of the enemy.* Paul said, "We are not ignorant of his devices" [II Corinthians 2:11]. "But the Helper, the Holy Spirit, whom the Father will send in My name, He will teach you all things, and bring to your remembrance all things that I said to you" [John 14:26].

We know that unlimited provisions have been set aside for our waging of war against Lucifer. "You did not choose Me, but I chose you and appointed you that you should go and bear fruit, and that your fruit should remain, that whatever you ask the Father in My name He may give you" [John 15:16].

"But you shall receive power when the Holy Spirit has come upon you; and you shall be witnesses to Me in Jerusalem, and in all Judea and Samaria, and to the end of the earth" [Acts 1:8].

"And He Himself gave some to be apostles, some prophets, some evangelists, and some pastors and teachers, for the equipping of the saints for the work of ministry, for the edifying of the body of Christ, till we all come to the unity of the faith and of the knowledge of the Son of God, to a perfect man, to the measure of the stature of the fullness of Christ; that we should no longer be children, tossed to and fro and carried about with every wind of doctrine, by the trickery of men, in the cunning craftiness of deceitful plotting, but, speaking the truth in love, may grow up in all things into Him who is the head—Christ—" [Ephesians 4:11-15].

3. *God observed the tragedy of Satan. He set in place the plan and intention that would save Man and erase from the universe all the evil of Satan.* "And I will put enmity between you and the woman, and between your seed and her Seed; He shall bruise your head, and you shall bruise His heel" [Genesis 3:15].

He assessed the situation. He made His estimates and found that it would cost the life of His Son. He took a stand and paid the price with His Son's life because somehow He found you and I worthy of His love. The Bible was created from that eternal why. ". . . just as He chose us in

Him before the foundation of the world, that we should be holy and without blame before Him in love, having predestined us to adoption as sons by Jesus Christ to Himself, according to the good pleasure of His will, to the praise of the glory of His grace, by which He made us accepted in the Beloved. In Him we have redemption through His blood, the forgiveness of sins, according to the riches of His grace which He made to abound toward us in all wisdom and prudence, having made known to us the mystery of His will, according to His good pleasure which He purposed in Himself, that in the dispensation of the fullness of the times He might gather together in one all things in Christ, both which are in heaven and which are on earth—in Him. In Him also we have obtained an inheritance, being predestined according to the purpose of Him who works all things according to the counsel of His will" [Ephesians 1:4-11].

4. *Jesus longs to reveal your individual assignment.* "I beseech you therefore, brethren, by the mercies of God, that you present your bodies a living sacrifice, holy, acceptable to God, which is your reasonable service. And do not be conformed to this world, but be transformed by the renewing of your mind, that you may prove what is that good and acceptable and perfect

will of God. For I say, through the grace given to me, to everyone who is among you, not to think of himself more highly than he ought to think, but to think soberly, as God has dealt to each one a measure of faith. For as we have many members in one body, but all the members do not have the same function, so we, being many, are one body in Christ, and individually members of one another" [Romans 12:2-5].

You and Jesus have an appointment. The purpose is to go all the way back to the core of your existence. It does no good to be built on The Rock if there are layers of silt between you and your foundation. The Holy Spirit wants to dig out all that is between you and Christ and make you immovable.

What we are after is certainty of our connection to Christ, to know that we are seated with Him in heavenly places. From that secure position, we view the world and interpret everything around us. We trust our Lord so completely that we embody His declaration of war on the Monarch of Evil.

We display the enmity of God toward Satan. This holy hatred fuels a life capable of sacrifice. We are done with the comfortable and the mundane. We see the end from the beginning. We realize the plan to which we are loyal cannot fail.

Our Bible is at once a battle plan of our unique assignment and a guarantee of victory. No other army in the universe can make such a boast.

These four factors not only must be present before war is declared, they also will keep the army on course and out of meaningless skirmishes and from wasting their resources once the war begins. Sun Tsu said that all war is deception. How many Christians do you know that are on the wrong battlefield?

Our greatest need at this moment is to drop everything we are doing and to assess whether or not we have even experienced a true conversion. This seems rather harsh, yet it is essential. Even Paul said to examine ourselves to see if we are "in the faith."

If we are clearly converted, we understand that we have signed our right to interpret life over to God. We have given ourselves to the Lordship of Christ. He has become our consciousness, our thoughts, and our interpretation of all that goes on around us. We allow God to be our compass, our director, and the captain of our salvation. We understand the end from the beginning because we are tapped into He who wrote the end from the beginning.

By knowing the end from the beginning, you are able to judge your life and work backwards to where you are. At this moment, understanding that victory is inevitable and that ultimately every attack of Satan is futile, you then understand how Satan got where he got. You understand your enemy, as a soldier must in war. You will see that everything he does is calculated to backfire. What is most important is that you will know how to respond to his attacks.

Why has the Church produced such weak soldiers? Why have we not marched forward in war as an undivided regiment of mighty men and women of God? We lack intention. We lack purpose. Too much of our Christian faith is rooted in carnal pleasure. The moment we face our first test, most of us cannot keep going because we do not see the more real, invisible world. Our objective, according to the Word of God, is that we are to "Go into all the world and preach the gospel." Why we have not gone in power, in unity, and without breaking ranks is made obvious by the fact that we do not have an overwhelming core *why* for our lives.

God has placed within your grasp an indescribable power, the power to grow, the power to know why you exist, and to know why you believe what you believe. You can catch a ride on the driving force of the whole universe. Never again will you need to be bewildered by mixed signals, because your inner compass will keep you on track. Never again will you have to cave in to times of adversity or suffering, because you have already traveled into the future and have seen the results of your trials.

"For I consider that the sufferings of this present time are not worthy to be compared with the glory which shall be revealed in us" [Romans 8:18].

Your enemy cannot do any of these things: he cannot evolve, improve, or draw upon future hope. For you, there is not just the *why*, but the focused reason, your individual part in the battle plan. The moment you accept your special assignment from God, you are connected to the world-wide acts of the Holy Spirit.

In every generation, the regions of Hell belch out some new device which is meant to damn souls in mass. God Almighty always anticipates this and forges His own weapons to nullify the vile influence of our enemy.

All power, meaning, and purpose is waiting for you. God stands ready to make you a weapon for this moment in history. As I said before, you are to be seated with Christ in heavenly places. What an astonishing difference it will make when you begin to look at your life from this vantage point! You will make excellent choices. Walls of doubt will become speed bumps. You will become the dread of demons. Most of all, you will be clothed in the sense of the rightness of your intention. Nothing will stop you! The outside world will notice and respond.

The fact is, when we really know *why we preach what we preach*, the world will sense *why they should listen.*

—Martin

Conation

The Violent Take It By Force

Dear Warrior,

You are about to unlock one of the most wonderful insights in the world, but it is also very dangerous.

First I must ask you a question: *How important is it to act on truth?* We all know people who have good intentions but never seem to turn those intentions into actions. We don't consider it a major fault because it is so common. Now let me enlarge the question: *How crucial is it for you to implement a truth God has revealed?* Now the issue takes a quantum leap.

Compelling truth that is believed but not performed becomes the most lethal lie we ever experience. That interlude between revelation and action is life and death. It is an incontrovertible fact that the longer a truth lingers, the more likely it is to lose its power to change us.

Satan attacks right after birth. He went after Moses and Jesus while they were still babies. Observe the Dragon in Revelation 12:1-4:

"Now a great sign appeared in heaven: a woman clothed with the sun, with the moon under her feet, and on her head a garland of twelve stars. Then being with child, she cried out in labor and in pain to give birth. And another sign appeared in heaven: behold, a great, fiery red dragon having seven heads and ten horns, and seven diadems on his heads. His tail drew a third of the stars of heaven and threw them to the earth. And the dragon stood before the woman who was ready to give birth, to devour her Child as soon as it was born."

The Evil One will lay back and allow a truth to be born in you, but then he will pounce on it while it is still in the halfway house. That is a key moment. But an unused truth does not simply rattle around in you harmlessly. It changes into a toxic substance. First, it erodes your identity: "For if anyone is a hearer of the word and not a doer, he is like a man observing his natural face in a mirror; for he observes himself, goes away, and immediately forgets what kind of man he was" [James 1:23-24].

Next, if it is not checked, it can create a second condition that is infinitely more dangerous, where the line between belief and action is badly blurred. People become spectators who seek the thrill of learning a new principle, but they will not make it happen. "For the time will come when they will not endure sound doctrine, but according to their own desires, because they have itching ears, they will heap up for themselves teachers; and they will turn their ears away from the truth and be turned aside to fables" [II Timothy 4:3-4]. They are not aware that they are not carrying it out because they think the thrill itself is a complete act.

Many preachers cater to this kind of audience, people who love to "ooh" and "ah" at well-stated insights but leave worse off than before.

Jehovah warned Ezekiel about this crowd: "So they come to you as people do, they sit before you as My people, and they hear your words, but they do not do them: for with their mouth they show much love, but their hearts pursue their own gain. Indeed you are to them as a very lovely song of one who has a pleasant voice and can play well on an instrument; for they hear your words, but they do not do them" [Ezekiel 33:31-32].

Look around you. They are everywhere. Believers are on church life support machines. They are never out of danger. They are weak and self-centered. The constant maintenance this breed requires has sapped leaders, gobbled up resources, and ultimately forced the army of God off the battlefield. Our methods and traditions have helped the Devil create an entire generation that is informed but not transformed.

Later you will see in totality what conation is, but for now you must simply see it as *an explosive desire to act on the voice of God.* It is present when spiritual discovery is made. It is a natural part of the Holy Spirit's work.

Here is a key factor in our current disaster: our methods and priorities in church discourage and even *fight* conation. For example, when a church leader, who is trying to make an impression on a culture, deliberately tries to stop a person who is "getting emotional" in an act of repentance. When the leader stops this person, they do a double disservice: first, they hinder the work of the Holy Spirit by interfering with true transformation in a person, and second, they limit the power and scope of their own ministry. It is ironic that they want dignity to attract the right crowd, not knowing that if they get it, that crowd will ungratefully use them up!

On the other hand, if they stay out of the Spirit's way, they will create disciples who are on fire and who will reproduce their own kind. Soon the Church will overflow, and this breed of disciple will make their pastor's life a joy!

Conation is so much more than this. Look at a fuller definition: *Conation, in psychology, is the area of one's active mentality that has to do with desire, volition, and striving. It is the energy of the mind which produces an effort.*

But the Holy Ghost version is infinitely more than this. It is a violent, God-given drive to succeed in the pursuit of a divine goal. It doesn't back down, back up, back off, or back away! It says, in essence, you will have to kill me to stop me. It is raw, holy enthusiasm, excitement, dynamic drive, and fire in the bones. It is pure initiative that propels someone into a single-minded pursuit of a vision.

Jesus said, "The zeal of your house has eaten me up." The first secret of the God-Warrior is his *'why'* or intention. The second secret is *conation*—the fire that ignites the *why*.

Conation is naturally present in young believers. It is either fanned into flames or smothered by the mediocre, entertainment leaders who will dispense truth in doses that don't revolutionize, but immunize instead.

Do you really want to damage the Devil? Begin by renouncing the possibility that you will ever have a belief without an action. Purpose and conation can never be separated in you again.

Above all, conation is a matter of choice. We can increase our appetites for victory. The great missionary to China, Arthur Mathews, said, "We are only as victorious as we want to be.

Lack of inner victory cannot be blamed on anyone but ourselves. Each man has his own measuring cup and measures out the quantity of victory he desires. Beyond that, for some perverse reason, we will not stretch ourselves. Today the message of victory is being misrepresented, cheapened, and deluted by Christians who are content with lowered standards and limited victory because in their hearts, they do not really want victory.["][3]

Many people who are well educated, intelligent, likable, and talented do not have this fire. This means that they will experience defeat when they least expect it. Look at a king who had everything but the conative force:

"Elisha had become sick with the illness of which he would die. Then Joash the king of Israel came down to him, and wept over his face, and said, 'O my father, my father, the chariots of Israel and their horsemen!' And Elisha said to him. 'Take a bow and some arrows.' So he took himself a bow and some arrows. The he said to the king of Israel, 'Put your hand on the bow'; So he put his hand on it, and Elisha put his hands on the king's hands. And he said, 'Open the east window'; and he opened it. Then Elisha said, 'Shoot,' and he shot. And he said, 'The arrow of the Lord's deliverance is the arrow of deliverance from Syria; for you must strike the Syrians at Aphek till you have destroyed them.'

Then he said, 'Take the arrows'; so he took them. And he said to the king of Israel, 'Strike the ground'; so he struck three times, and stopped. And the man of God was angry with him, and said, 'You should have struck five or six times, then you would have struck Syria till you had destroyed it! But now you will strike Syria only three times'" [II Kings 13:14-19].

The prophet Elisha gave the king clear steps to follow in order to find victory. They are there for us as well.

1. *"Get a bow and some arrows."* When you grab a weapon, you demonstrate your intention to fight. All of your anger towards the Devil, all of your claims of compassion for oppressed people, is just talk until you take up your weapon. Begin by taking the Sword of the Spirit against your own sin and contentment and compromise.

2. *"Take the bow in your hands . . . and Elisha put his hands on the king's hands."* No matter how weak you feel at this moment, no matter how lacking in true fire you believe you are, the moment you put your hand to the weapon God has given you, he will put His hand over yours, surging conation into your very being.

3. *"Open the window eastward and shoot."* The big *why* in our life has located the

enemy and the point of attack. The arrow is our heart, headed toward that battle-field.

4. *"Beat on the ground."* The prophet tested the king's conation. The king revealed his appetite for victory. He decided the size of the victory. Sadly, the fire simply was not there. After three "love taps," he stopped. Though he was promised victory through prophecy he derailed the divine strategy by a lack of appetite for war and triumph.

Once again we must see an axiom of war. Sun Tzu said about a victorious general: "He gains victory by seizing opportunity without hesitation."[4] The true warrior is conative!

Conation in war is called *the offensive*. The army that is first to take the initiative and attack always has the advantage. The general who is on the attack has an edge; he has made his decisions first and then carries them out. In essence, he has set the rules for the engagement. An enemy is forced to wait and see what the attacker is doing before he can make any decision.

David practiced this principle when he faced Goliath. Anyone would expect a boy pitted against a giant to duck and dodge. But David ran toward Goliath. By doing so, he forced the goon to react, and that momentary edge was all the boy needed to send the pebble on its historic flight.

In war, conation takes on two exceedingly crucial elements: *first is the willingness of the army to fire their weapons; this is an attitude.* Any military expert will tell you that the ability and will to use weapons is what warfare is all about. Many well-equipped battalions have marched out to fight and then lost the battle because, at the time of attack, they froze up and simply did not have the will to fire their weapons. Having a weapon and using a weapon are not the same thing. We may be able to hit a bulls-eye on the firing range, but that is useless if, during the attack, we fail to pull the trigger.

We have the ultimate weapons: "For though we walk in the flesh, we do not war according to the flesh. For the weapons of our warfare are not carnal but mighty in God for pulling down strongholds . . ." [II Corinthians 10:3-4].

The Christian Church has proven that it can have the ultimate weapons and still not fire them upon society's ills. It is the next verse that reveals the conation:

". . . casting down arguments and every high thing that exalts itself against the knowledge of God, bringing every thought into captivity to the obedience of Christ . . ." [II Corinthians 10:5].

The attacker-heart casts down and takes captive.

The second crucial element of conation is the obsession to get to a meaningful target and deliver the decisive blow. Jomini said, "In either case it should be well understood that there is, in every battlefield, a decisive point which more than any other helps to secure the victory by enabling its holder to make proper application of the principles of war. Arrangements should therefore be made for striking the decisive blow upon this point."[5]

God is conative. He sees the evil of our day. He has made His estimates for victory. He has written His plan for triumph, and He has chosen the decisive target. He is now seeking to instill His own *will to win* in those who are willing to accept. He will then reveal the target to them. God's army does not belong in safe havens, but invading the nests where the Evil One hatches his schemes.

This class of conative Christian is the one Daniel referred to when he looked into the future through the eyes of God and said, "But the people who know their God will be strong and carry out great exploits" [Daniel 11:32b].

So, if conation is anything, it is, in essence, the dynamite of God to carry out an exploit.

Once Jesus was asked to explain the astonishing awakening that John the Baptist ignited, possibly a quarter of a million people were baptized into his message of fiery repentance. Jesus said, what is, in some ways, still considered a mystery, "From John the Baptist until now, the kingdom of God suffers violence, and the violent take it by force" [Matthew 11:12].

One of the implications here is that mass revival is a weather pattern. Vacuums catalyze hurricane winds as nature rushes in to fill a void.

The Spirit world has the same phenomenon. Grinding immorality empties out a generation's spirit. They become starved for what has been drained out of them. Notice in II Timothy 3, four words beginning with the prefix "un" that describe end-time evil: unthankful, unholy, unloving, and unforgiving. "Un," we all know, means *without*. These souls are bereft of gratitude, holiness, forgiveness, and love.

When the awesome *why* of God is dropped on parched souls, people will forcefully invade the kingdom which is no longer hidden. Masses realize that what is being poured out by God is precisely what they are starved for, and they will take it by force.

When you have a soul with a voracious appetite for life, and an aggressive, loving God moving toward that soul, it brings about a hurricane effect that nothing can stop. Demons, hypocrites, and mediocre by-standers will be trampled by the inevitable stampede.

God needs captains, warriors, and vessels to start the storm! Why not you? Why not let this great gift of conation—victory fuel—find combustion in your soul? When God sees one of His own declare himself a warrior, by taking up weapons to attempt the impossible, He drops what He is doing and rushes in, bringing the host of heaven with Him to help divide and conquer and rout the enemy.

You know better than to wait. Conation tells you that there is no need or point in waiting for some missing element, additional training, or perfected talent. You can and must begin now! Common in every defeat of Satan is the unashamed enforcement of the Word of God and the implementation of it as the absolute truth in a direct confrontation against the lies, distortions, and perversions of the Evil One.

How much victory do you want? Do you want to "love tap" the arrows of deliverance? Or smash the ground again and again until the malignant, mediocre life is dead and you are consumed by an unbearable need to attack?

You know God's intention. You know the evil that is at work. It is clear to you what Satan has done in creating Christians who are so comatose with doctrines and beliefs that they are oblivious to their disobedience.

You know the pulpiteers who do not preach to revolutionize, but to sustain their own careers. You have seen believers sing, chant, and shout victory. They carry on as if something meaningful is going on. They passionately affirm their desire to make a difference, but it is all a well-choreographed dance of fear. They hope to kick up enough dust so that no one notices they have not gone off to war.

Remember, the attackers always have the edge in war. They have clarified their objectives. They have found their assigned places. The attackers have control and possess the power to change the situation. They choose when and where the fight will begin.

This instantly puts the enemy on the defensive. The enemy cannot decide what to do until the attack is started. They cannot choose what part of their army will be attacked. Sun Tzu said, "Let not there be lengthy campaigns, but let our objective be victory."

The victory-obsessed army streamlines. They are not enthralled by maneuvers and military operations. They want a direct course to conquest.

Allow me one last illustration of conation. "Now Moses was tending the flock of Jethro his father-in-law, the priest of Midian. And he led the flock to the back of the desert, and came to Horeb, the mountain of God" [Exodus 3:1]. Moses is herding sheep! Here is "the man for the ages" who will walk with God and will lead two million Jews through a parted sea into their promised land, but at this point, he is only leading livestock.

Then the Bible tells us in Exodus 3:2-3, "And

the Angel of the Lord appeared to him in a flame of fire from the midst of a bush. So he looked, and behold, the bush was burning with fire, but the bush was not consumed. Then Moses said, 'I will now turn aside and see this great sight, why the bush does not burn.'" He wanted to know *why*! He had no inkling of how gigantic the *why* was that he was about to embrace!

Let me ask you the question that Moses asked. *Why didn't the bush burn up?* To be sure, it was a sign, but it was also a message. The fire of God needs no fuel. It is totally self-sustaining.

Moses knew that what he was seeing transcended physical law. Moses's fire, on the other hand, had gone out. He had run from his destiny. He had failed and even murdered an Egyptian in a bungled rescue mission. This burned-out man could never trust in the fuel of his emotion again. But there before him was what he desperately needed. The fire of the bush would be his fire to fulfill the *why*!

God was saying to Moses, "Partake of my conative nature." With it, Moses could go and complete his work, crossing the finish line with fire left over.

You, my friend, are right there, right now, ready to embody a fire that doesn't need the propellant of good moods, promising situations, fair weather, the praises of men, or any such thing to keep going. Fire that, in the absence of any fuel, keeps burning, and burning, and burning. Through all crises, heartache, fear, and disappointment, the flame never goes out until you have reached the enemy target and destroyed it completely. That is conation.

Do not sit there wishing you were powerful, effective, or making a big difference. Get up right now! Take it by force!

— Martin

The Steel Punch

Dear Warrior,

Imagine someone taking his hands and striking an opponent with fingers dangling. He would hurt himself more than his adversary! This is a sadly accurate picture of the Christian movement. With depressing frequency, we have attacked with disjointed leadership, limp weapons, and wilting warriors. This is why our efforts have damaged us more than Satan. We seem to know how to do everything but make a fist.

What heightens this tragedy is that it is so avoidable. History is replete with episodes of totally unlikely heroes who, permeated by God, without warning, delivered a knock-out punch to Lucifer.

David saw God's *steel punch* up close in a stunning victory that came out of nowhere.

He was so awed by this shocking deliverance that, to honor God, he named the site of the victory, Baal Perazim, meaning "Master of Breakthroughs."

Breakthrough is a noble word of war that has been cheapened by overuse. A breakthrough is a decisive blow at the front line. It is the turning point of a war, where the enemy's line of defense has been breeched, and warriors are flooding in to take strategic territory.

The *steel punch* is a gift from God that causes breakthroughs in demonic strongholds. This uniquely powerful gift obliterates the works of the Devil. Here is our great problem, however. We do not strike evil where it matters, and we do not seek meaningful targets.

By now I hope you are rabid to attack Satan, and that you want to do serious damage to meaningful targets. Have you internalized the surpassing purpose of the Almighty? Is that purpose on fire within you? If so, then your next logical step is acquiring the *steel punch* of God.

How can you obtain this gift? Start by realizing that a whole lot more than shouting brought down the walls of Jericho! This story is the essence of how God makes a fist. The Israelites marched around the city as often as Joshua commanded. They never broke ranks and maintained an eerie silence. However, they were making a fearsome sound in the spirit world.

They were attacking where it mattered. Through their obedience, they bombarded the invisible until the fist was formed. The shout delivered the blow. The battlements of evil were so totally gutted already that the collapsing physical walls were only a formality.

The Book of Acts records its own version of this potent punch. In Phillipi, Paul and Silas are locked up. They had no means of escape and no way to fight back. At midnight, they unleashed the song of the Lord. Once again, God bared His knuckles and the jailhouse quaked and crumbled. It was totally destroyed. Chains fell off the prisoners and yet no one was hurt. Like Jericho, this was a *Spirit-victory* that suddenly turned physical.

You have some very crucial questions to answer before you can progress any further: (1) Does God want to give you the *steel punch*? (2) Will you know what to do with it? My heart says a violent "yes" to both questions.

Jehovah reiterates His zeal to arm and mentor willing warriors all through scripture. David said, "He trains my hand for war" [Psalm 18:34]. This certainty must pervade you. You must see how natural it is for you to step into this gift.

The *steel punch* is known as something else in the annals of war. It is called the *principle of concentration*. Sun Tsu describes the wise general this way, ". . . he marches with divine swift-ness; his blows fall like thunderbolts, 'from the nine-layered heavens.' He creates conditions cer-tain to produce a quick decision."[6] *Concentra-tion is the calculated massing of overwhelming force at a decisive point in order to obtain a breakthrough.*

Warlords of all time have concluded that there are four universal features of concen-tration:

1. *You must choose a target that is both feasi-ble and important.*
   A. It must be a feasible target because it is a mistake to attack a heavily fortified po-sition where you have no hope of break-through.
   B. It must be an important target because it is a waste to attack a weak position where no meaningful damage to the enemy is done.
2. *The attack must be focused so that it is overwhelming even if you are outnumbered.*
3. *The attack must be original in appearance, but classical in application.*
4. *You must weaken the non-essential points of your defense to amass personnel at the decisive point.*

These same four laws make up God's *steel*

punch. Follow me as I apply these to God's army and to you in particular.

1. *We must choose the right place to attack.*
   A. Once again, we must choose a target that is feasible. For us, feasibility means that we have received a word from God. For we know that "if God is for us, who can be against us?" [Romans 8:31b] But feasibility is not just an issue of God's authority but of our own level of faith and the depth of the fight "within us." Caleb said, "Let us go up at once and take possession, for we are well able to overcome it" [Numbers 13:30].
   B. *It must be a meaningful target.* It is an ugly waste of resources for the Church to attack Satan at an uncontested point since it will not lead to a spiritual breakthrough. All too often the modern Church has become a "master of illusion" that, like Don Quixote, tilts windmills and calls them mortal enemies. We have done a lot of posturing, but exceedingly little penetration. We have, as a result of this, bred doubt in our youth, who know our targets are not meaningful and that our antics belie our claims of might.

Paul renounced these war games when he

said, "Therefore I run thus: not with uncertainty. Thus I fight: not as one who beats the air" [I Corinthians 9:26].

Let me now present you with an example of how this worked in our warfare for men's souls in China. In my ministry I faced racism that wounded my heart. We were winning the poor people of our village because they were open and humble. The social class that our missions board wanted us to reach were arrogant and belligerent toward the gospel. I refused to meet this racial quota and to cater to the wealthy. Instead, I won the poor and minorities in vast numbers. This decisive point was a correct choice for these reasons: first, the people we chose to minister to were a feasible target, and secondly, they were a meaningful target, because once they were converted they were so full of fire and gratitude that they caused breakthroughs at all levels of society.

There are many American churches that overlook people who have no money and no station in society. This is horrendous! These people are poor, simple, and lonely. They are available targets for the gospel message and are strategically positioned for a breakthrough against Satan.

How quickly we forget what God promised and warned us He would do in I Corinthians 1:27-28: "But God has chosen the foolish things of the world to put to shame the wise, and God has chosen the weak things of the world to put to shame the things which are mighty; and the base things of the world and the things which are despised God has chosen, and the things which are not, to bring to nothing the things that are." It is evident that those who are poor and lowly have been chosen of God to be a *steel punch* to nullify the arrogant wise of the world. In this way, no one will be glorified but God.

2. *Our attack must be focused and overwhelming even if we are outnumbered.* It is strange, but true, that the airplane went through two major wars before it was a factor as a weapon. The reason for this is that it was not used in concentration. Remember, no matter how new or how lethal a weapon is, it will not be effective until it is engaged according to the laws of war.

Major General Claire Chennault is credited with being the first to use the airplane in concentration. Jim Wilson said, "When he (Chennault) went to Burma and China, his pilots stuck together. Outnumbered in the air and on the ground in planes, pilots, and parts, they destroyed 217 enemy planes and probably 43 more with a maximum of 20 operational P-40s in 31 encounters."[7] Chennault's losses were six pilots and sixteen planes. In order to accomplish this, Chennault used concentration. He simply had two aircraft firing at one enemy aircraft. Even if outnumbered in the air 10 to 1, Chennault's two always outnumbered the enemy's one.

For you and me, this explains why Jesus sent the disciples out two by two. "After these things the Lord appointed seventy others also, and sent them two by two before His face into every city and place where He Himself was about to go. Then He said to them, The harvest truly is great, but the laborers are few; therefore pray the Lord of the harvest to send out laborers into His harvest" [Luke 10:1-2].

There is overpowering evidence in the Bible that God has teamed up warriors: We see Moses and Aaron, Caleb and Joshua, David and Jonathan, Peter and James, and Paul and Silas. Look at Matthew 18:19-20. "Again I say to you that if two of you agree on earth concerning anything that they ask, it will be done for them by My Father in heaven. For where two or three are gathered together in My name, I am there in the midst of them." This is a prayer of concentration!

When two march, pray, and bear one another's burdens, they become that force that the Bible acclaims: "And two put ten thousand to flight" [Deuteronomy 32:30]. But even that record was broken by Jonathan and his armor bearer who sent hundreds of thousands to flight in I Samuel 14. Look at the key proclamation in I

Samuel 14:6: "Then Jonathan said to the young man who bore his armor, 'Come, let us go over to the garrison of these uncircumcised; it may be that the Lord will work for us. For nothing restrains the Lord from saving by many or few.'"

These glorious words show the whole picture of concentration and their expectation of the *steel punch*. Find your partner, focus your prayer, and attack together. Even if a million demons come against you, they will still have to face two of you to every one of them.

3. *The attack must be original in appearance, but classical in application.*

Christians are such copycats! Whenever we have a chance to do something fresh, we immediately imitate each other. We must stage events outside of church buildings and at times that are other than on Sunday mornings. This confuses Satan. Our singers and artists must go beyond just emulating *pop* music to get an audience. Concentration means being bold enough to have an original voice that sets secular society on its ear. Pastors should stop deriving their tactics from the buzz trends of the day and instead obtain creative attack modes from the Holy Spirit.

Someone said that insanity is doing the same thing over and over again expecting a different result. Let's wake up! *If we want to get results that we have never had before, we must do things we have never done before.*

Whenever possible, God does something new. That's the passion of the Creator. We are commanded to "sing a new song"; we are commissioned to "bring forth fruit." That means it wasn't there before and it wasn't done that way before. I am convinced that the reason it seems that God is not talking to us is because we are listening for Him to repeat Himself when, in fact, He is trying to say something new.

God longs for the fresh approach that is rooted in classical truth. This new breed of attack will not violate scripture, but in fact, reinforce it.

4. *You must weaken the non-essential points of your defense in order to attack at the decisive point.*

This is very important to you. Satan relies on deception. He wants you to believe that you do not have time or resources to attack. Look again. You will see saboteurs robbing you of both time and resources.

Many Christians believe that "getting right with God" means we stop doing bad things. But the warrior stops doing good things if necessary to make way for doing the excellent thing.

The purpose of land mines and booby traps is to implement passive resistance so that an army can move its soldiers and equipment to the decisive point. That is exactly what you must do. Say "no" to flaky friends, guilt-inducing relatives, and a host of decent, but distracting activities.

Daniel knew that he had to focus and attack Babylon through prayer. He had to make room for that by saying "no." "But Daniel purposed in his heart that he would not defile himself with the portion of the king's delicacies, nor with the wine which he drank; therefore he requested of the chief of the eunuchs that he might not defile himself" [Daniel 1:8].

You must deliberately weaken projects that seem compelling but stop you from forming the *steel punch*. My dear warrior, flee from the deception of daily life and get somewhere where you can make decisions. Let God show you who your co-worker is, the one who will multiply your attack strength. Get ready for shock weapons and tactics. Get ready to have a single moment of irresistible power that will bring the breakthrough that you and God so deeply yearn to see.

—Martin

SECRET #4

Godspeed!

"He Marches with Divine Swiftness"
—Sun Tzu

Dear Warrior,

Get your Bible! Open it to Acts 16:6-8. "Now when they had gone through Phrygia and the region of Galatia, they were forbidden by the Holy Spirit to preach the word in Asia. After they had come to Mysia, they tried to go into Bithynia, but the Spirit did not permit them. So passing by Mysia, they came down to Troas." Here you find your next secret.

Look carefully. What you see is a weapon of God (the Apostle Paul) that refuses to be static. He is not passively swooning in the hope that Jesus will use him. He is, in fact, bouncing from one door to the next expecting coordinates to damage the Devil!

Paul beds down in Troas, and wham! a vision appears: "And a vision appeared to Paul in the night. A man of Macedonia stood and pleaded with him, saying, 'Come over to Macedonia and help us.' Now after he had seen the vision, immediately we sought to go to Macedonia, concluding that the Lord had called us to preach the gospel to them" [Acts 16:9-10]. Now he knows his assignment; he knows where the *steel punch* will be delivered and he wastes no time heading to that decisive point.

Paul is now a heat-seeking missile. But God is throwing in a miracle that isn't even emphasized in this account in Acts. "Therefore, sailing from Troas, we ran a straight course to Samothrace, and the next day came to Neapolis, and from there to Philippi, which is the foremost city of that part of Macedonia, a colony" [Acts 16:11-12a]. It takes a boat more than two days to sail from Troas to Samothrace, but Paul, Silas and Timothy made it in less than one!

What happened? Well, on very rare occasions a wind would rise up in that region that would cut the time to less than half of normal. God sent that wind and they sailed with *godspeed*.

All of the secrets that I have mentioned so far are at work in this account of Paul. He is possessed of purpose (*why*). He is relentless in his determination (*conation*). He has discovered the place of attack (*steel punch*). And now, Secret

#4 is called *godspeed.* Each secret builds on and is at the mercy of the previous one.

It is useless to have a giant why for your life if there is no fire to fulfill it! But then, if you have the fire and no weapon or attack point, you are still helpless! Now even when all of that is present, you must *go.* You must get there. Getting there is what this entire letter is about.

Our next example, Simon Peter, shows us that we sometimes need a violent change before we can go. "Then he became very hungry and wanted to eat; but while they made ready, he fell into a trance and saw heaven opened and an object like a great sheet bound at the four corners, descending to him and let down to the earth. In it were all kinds of four-footed animals of the earth, wild beasts, creeping things, and birds of the air. And a voice came to him, 'Rise, Peter: kill and eat.' But Peter said, 'Not so, Lord! For I have never eaten anything common or unclean.' And a voice spoke to him again the second time, 'What God has cleansed you must not call common.' This was done three times. And the object was taken up into heaven again. Now while Peter wondered within himself what this vision which he had seen meant, behold, the men who had been sent from Cornelius had made inquiry for Simon's house, and stood before the gate. And they called and asked whether Simon, whose surname was Peter, was lodging there. While Peter thought about the vision, the Spirit said to him, 'Behold, three men are seeking you. Arise therefore, go down and go with them, doubting nothing; for I have sent them'" [Acts 10:10-20].

Let me assure you that Peter had passed the tests of the first three secrets with flying colors. But now he is stuck. This vision is not about revealing his point of attack but the racism that would keep him from going! The bottom line of the vision? *"Go down and go with them."*

The word *go* is mightier than we know. You can't appreciate how revolutionary Jesus is until you realize that when He said, "Go into all the world," He went in the radically opposite direction of virtually every other religious figure in history. All of the rest ordered their devotees to stay, or retire to monasteries, or meditate or isolate themselves to atone for their inner corruptions and hide from evil.

In essence Jesus said, "Go global, keep moving, grow as you go, and remember, I prayed that the Evil One will be kept from you so you can be *'in the world but not of it.'* The Helper will take you each step of the way."

The gift of *godspeed* is far more than quickness or momentum; it is a gift that is physical because we become a quick study of our Enemy, and it is spiritual because we can travel to attack points in prayer faster than Satan and faster than light.

Once again you see a principle of war. This one is called *mobility*. Mobility was the centerpiece of Sun Tzu's training. He said, "What is of the greatest importance in war is extraordinary speed."[8]

This becomes evident when you define the word *immobilized*. An army that has been stripped of movement is at the total disposal of its adversary. It cannot attack or retreat. It can only stand and wait for disaster.

Sun Tzu saw mobility as four separate facets:

1. *Mobility is getting to the battleline first.* "Generally, he who occupies the field of battle first and awaits his enemy is at ease; he who comes later to the scene and rushes into the fight is weary."[9] This edge is obvious. A rested, entrenched army that has time to watch you arrive has won the mental battle.

2. *Mobility is the quickness to see danger and instantly move out of harm's way.* Sun Tzu said, "The wise general cannot be manipulated. He may withdraw, but when he does, he moves so quickly that he cannot be overtaken."[10] Mobility is in the mind and spirit of a general as much as it is in the feet of his soldiers. He puts his ego aside and reverses course when danger demands it, but he will so outrun his enemy that at some point, he will turn and counterattack with lightning-like quickness.

3. *Mobility is flexibility*. In war, adjustment is constant and change is sudden. How fast an army adapts to change is also mobility. Sun Tzu said, "If wise, a commander is able to recognize changing circumstances and act expediently."[11] The ultimate form of mobility is when a leader can turn an army on its heels and get it to alter its attack strategy to seize opportunities that arise.

Sun Tzu reiterates flexibility by comparing a mobilized army to water. "And as water shapes its flow in accordance with the ground, so an army manages its victory in accordance with the situation of the enemy. And as water has no constant form, there are in war no constant conditions. Thus, one able to gain the victory by modifying his tactics in accordance with the enemy's situation may be said to be divine."[12]

4. *Mobility is range and scope*. With mobility a little army looks big. It can traverse terrain quickly and be at an attack point of its choosing. Then all at once it can appear somewhere else giving the attacker a massive appearance.

This "look of scope" makes the enemy spread their defenses. Sun Tzu declared, "The enemy must not know where I intend to give battle. For if he does not know where I intend to give battle he must prepare in a great many places. And when he prepares in a great many places, those I have to fight in any one place will be few."[13]

So then, *mobility is an army's ability to get there, get back, get through, get around, and get over. It is swiftness, wisdom, flexibility, endurance, and elusiveness.* Sun Tzu summed it all up: "When campaigning, be swift as the wind; in leisurely march, majestic as the forest; in raiding and plundering, like fire; in standing, firm as the mountains. As unfathomable as the clouds, move like a thunderbolt."[14]

So then, if that is mobility, what is *godspeed*? As much as the Holy Spirit exceeds the wisdom of man, so does the supernatural power of *godspeed* exceed military mobility. Remember, there is no difference between physical and spiritual war. It is all war, and mobility is a human mirror image of *godspeed*.

Here are the four features of *godspeed*.

1. *Getting to the battleline first!* Unlike a physical warrior, you can get to the battleline through prayer. Godly warriors know that they can move faster than Satan or light! At dawn we can rise up and run to the decisive point as demons make their bid for control of the day.

How sad that we have forgotten this holy right to tear down strongholds by taking our position in the heavenlies. We can arrive rested and entrenched and attack the heart of the Enemy.

How awesome when our prayers mature beyond frantic crisis management, where we are begging God to clean up our messes! How mighty to instead be taking new territory in Jesus's Name!

But not only this—we go! It is silly to pray for a thing and not go and win it. Paul had to get somewhere and so do you! *Godspeed* is the gift of those who go. Those who seek clear guidance must understand: *God will not direct the static or passive*. Details are given to the mobilized! The *steel punch* cannot be delivered without momentum!

The priests were instructed in Joshua 3:13: "And it shall come to pass, as soon as the soles of the feet of the priests who bear the ark of the Lord, the Lord of all the earth, shall rest in the waters of the Jordan, that the waters of the Jordan shall be cut off, the waters that come down from upstream, and they shall stand as a heap."

The lepers also were ordered to go! "So when He saw them, He said to them, 'Go, show yourselves to the priests.' And so it was that as they went, they were cleansed" [Luke 17:14].

There is a time value to obedience. Demons are trying to solidify their hold, but God keeps the door open waiting for his fighters to arrive.

2. *Sensing danger and retreating.* God-warriors do not linger in temptation. They never test their strength against lust—they run! Joseph

did not even let Potiphar's wife finish her seductive sentence. ". . . she caught him by his garment, saying, 'Lie with me.' But he left his garment in her hand, and fled and ran outside" [Genesis 39:13-15].

Paul chose his words carefully to his "son in the Lord," Timothy. When it came to lust, he did *not* instruct him to be strong, overcome, or to take his stand. What he said was, "Flee also youthful lusts; but pursue righteousness, faith, love, peace with those who call on the Lord out of a pure heart" [II Timothy 2:22].

Godspeed is quick withdrawal from anger, jealousy, pride, and fear. A true gauge of your condition is how much time lapses between a crisis and prayer.

Godspeed is fast reaction to commitments that violate our objective! It is withdrawing from people who drag down your zeal. "But we command you, brethren, in the name of our Lord Jesus Christ, that you withdraw from every brother who walks disorderly and not according to the tradition which he received from us" [II Thessalonians 3:6].

And finally, *godspeed* is anything that affects our pace in the race. "Therefore we also, since we are surrounded by so great a cloud of witnesses, let us lay aside every weight, and the sin which so easily ensnares us and let us run with endurance the race that is set before us, looking unto Jesus, the author and finisher of our faith, who for the joy that was set before Him endured the cross, despising the shame, and has sat down at the right hand of the throne of God" [Hebrews 12:1-2].

3. *Divine flexibility.* Sometimes breakthroughs are delayed and we must pace ourselves for a long resistance. Other times it may come so fast and so big that we must make room for it by dropping our plans and running with the unexpected. We are "ready in season and out of season" [II Timothy 4:3].

As we move forward, we may find that the enemy is not outward devils, but inner attitudes. Remember what I said about Peter. Racism was broken by *godspeed,* and he was free to go with this sudden and historic breakthrough of the outpouring of the Spirit on the Gentiles. You must be aware of prejudices and biases that would stop you!

4. *Range and scope: this is your circle of authority.* Sun Tzu trained his men hard to be able to attack with range and speed in order to spread the enemy thin. We can again apply prayer to dizzy the Devil by attacking him along several fronts. But unlike a physical army, we have incredible power to increase our range and scope.

Paul wanted the church at Corinth to increase

their sphere of attack! "We, however, will not boast beyond measure, but within the limits of the sphere which God appointed us—a sphere which especially includes you. For we are not overextending ourselves (as though our authority did not extend to you), for it was to you that we came with the gospel of Christ; not boasting of things beyond measure, that is, in other men's labors, but having hope, that as your faith is increased, we shall be greatly enlarged by you in our sphere" [II Corinthians 10:13-15]. We can increase our prayers, enlarge the mobility of our outreaches, and attack with ever-increasing effectiveness.

Finally, my beloved warrior, let me sum up the matter. *Godspeed* is the crowning gift of a Holy Ghost mover! In II Kings 7, four lepers sat starving, waiting to die. They decide to do something desperate: "If we say, 'We will enter the city,' the famine is in the city, and we shall die there. And if we sit here, we die also. Now therefore, come, let us surrender to the army of the Syrians. If they keep us alive, we shall live; and if they kill us, we shall only die'" [II Kings 7:4].

Even though the lepers did not understand *godspeed*, they had just implemented it! This was all Jehovah was waiting for, for somebody to move toward the enemy! By now Heaven's fist was clenched and almost cramping.

Then a miracle happened! Whereas with Paul

it was a sailor's wind, here God provided a gloriously terrifying noise! "For the Lord had caused the army of the Syrians to hear the noise of chariots and the noise of horses—the noise of a great army; so they said to one another, 'Look, the king of Israel has hired against us the kings of the Hittites and the kings of the Egyptians to attack us!' Therefore they arose and fled at twilight, and left the camp intact—their tents, their horses, and their donkeys—and they fled for their lives" [II Kings 7:6-7]. Four dying lepers were not only mobilized to look bigger, they sounded invincible! The cold warrior hearts of the Syrians melted like water and they fled in all directions!

I know this sounds harsh, but I believe that God ignores those who want to be convinced that they should move to the battle front! He realizes that His purposes will just rattle around inside those people. God looks for people who are willing to put a deadline on their dream and their life on the line.

There are thousands of valid opportunities to inject the life-giving gospel! We have studied society long enough. We have crunched numbers long enough. We have lamented the crisis of youth long enough. God gives speed to righteously-moving feet. He sends wind to outstretched wings. God sits and wonders what part of "Go" we don't understand!

There is a demon watching you right now. I think he just flinched because you look like you are about to make your move.

— Martin

SECRET #5

Invincibility

Dear Warrior,

Here is my vote for the worst mistake the Christian movement has made in the last hundred years—the illusion that we can attack Satan and then make no allowance for his counterattack. Hear me well, warrior, if you have harmed Beelzebub, he will come after you!

The damage of what this immature view of war has done is beyond calculation. I believe the severest harm was that it pulled us off of the front line. We were stung after a great revival! Jonathan Edwards commented on why bizarre behavior chases true revival when he said, "When Satan sees that he cannot stop revival, he no longer opposes it, but instead he gets behind it so as to push it into emotional extremes."

In our ignorance, we gave the Devil a double victory: first, by destroying revival with the emotional abuses of some, and then by preventing future outpourings by the reaction of others who end up blaming revival itself for the abuses.

Escapist Christian leaders covered their desertion from the war by re-engineering the Christian life into a self-help journey and not a struggle against evil. The disaster is that at no point did Satan forget we were at war.

Still, these misled ministers fed an entire generation on a warless faith. Some even blobbed together secular positivism with bent verses. Victory was no longer defined as a legitimate assault on a demonic stronghold but a "rebuking away of all your problems as you learned to feel better about yourself."

When the army of God is healthy, it broadcasts a mighty light. Like a catalyst it changes the culture that surrounds it! But in sickness, the church absorbs the odor of the secular thinking near it.

Arthur Mathews said, "The thing that we need to be afraid of today is that the spirit that produces world trends should invade Christ's mighty army and argue us off the offensive into a compromised co-existence with the world's attitudes—so that we end up just like the world, taking lessons in French and practicing detente."[15]

This deplorable mistake is the costliest of all

time. How can we know the revivals it has aborted or the believers who have fallen because of it!

When it comes to Satan, the Christian who is casual becomes a casualty. Jim Wilson said, "Like any wise general, Satan will not attack a strong point if weak points are available for a breakthrough."[16]

You cannot toy with this unalterable fact: *at this moment you are either an available target or an available weapon.*

Now let us get to the point of this letter which is the fifth secret—*invincibility.*

"Finally, my brethren, be strong in the Lord and in the power of His might. Put on the whole armor of God, that you may be able to stand against the wiles of the devil. For we do not wrestle against flesh and blood, but against principalities, against powers, against the rulers of the darkness of this age, against spiritual hosts of wickedness in the heavenly places. Therefore take up the whole armor of God, that you may be able to withstand in the evil day, and having done all, to stand. Stand therefore, having girded your waist with truth, having put on the breastplate of righteousness, and having shod your feet with the preparation of the gospel of peace; above all, taking the shield of faith with which you will be able to quench all the fiery darts of the wicked one. And take the helmet of salvation, and the sword of the Spirit, which is the word of God" [Ephesians 6:10-17].

These timeless words are an order to become invincible, a warning against partial armor, and a promise of constant victory for the obedient.

Invincibility is the recognition that you are going to be attacked and you are ready! Jesus said, "The ruler of this world is coming and he has nothing in Me" [John 14:30].

Sun Tzu said, "Anciently the skillful warriors first made themselves invincible and awaited the enemy's moment of vulnerability."[17] Another translation of Sun Tzu indicates that they would first put themselves beyond the possibility of defeat.

That's my goal—to put you beyond the possibility of defeat! Do not misunderstand me. I am not talking about sinless perfection. That only comes in Heaven. What we are looking for is a condition that is promised to God's warriors where Satan is helpless.

Why would invincibility be the fifth secret and not an earlier one? It is because this gift shines on the front line where warriors are standing firm against return fire. This secret belongs to those who have put on armor. The only reason someone dons armor is because they are either looking for or expecting a fight.

Yet again there is a recognized principle of

war that is a natural reflection of invincibility; it is the principle of security.

Security is all the things a battalion does to erase the possibility of defeat. This is not just a precondition of war; it is ongoing. Once the war starts, security efforts intensify.

Generally most military experts divide security into three facets:

1. *Intelligence.* This is information about your enemy. Your spies and informants break codes, intercept communiques, and feed them back to you. You learn locations, times, and places of attack, strengths, and weaknesses. These are not prewar estimates but information that must come in continually and help you eliminate mistakes and find vulnerability in the enemy.

Sun Tzu said, "But vulnerability is not measured solely in physical terms. An opposing commander may be vacillating, rash, impulsive, arrogant, stubborn, or easily deceived. Possibly some elements of his army are poorly trained, disaffected, cowardly, or ineptly commanded. He may have selected a poor position. He may be over-extended, his supplies low, his troops exhausted. These conditions constitute voids and provide opportunity for an imaginative general to devise an advantageous course of action."[18]

But intelligence is not just finding out about

your enemy, it is making sure they are not finding out anything about you. True intelligence is when you know what your enemy looks like and what he is going to do but he remains ignorant about your intentions and conditions. Sun Tzu called this *shape*. " 'Shape him,' Sun Tzu says. Continuously concerned with observing and probing his opponent, the wise general at the same time takes every possible measure designed to prevent the enemy from 'shaping' him."[19]

2. *Fortification*. This is an encamped army on continuous watch. They are well hidden behind an impenetrable wall. They use fences, guards, traps, radar, and a host of other methods to detect intruders. But this is not a passive resistance. They are ready to attack on command. Sun Tzu's comment: "The experts in defense conceal themselves as under the ninefold earth; those skilled in attack move as from above the ninefold heavens. Thus they are capable both of protecting themselves and of gaining a complete victory."[20]

3. *The Final Stand*. This is the condition where an army knows it can take any attack thrown at them and then counterattack right afterwards. It is a core conviction that whenever or however it happens, they will meet and defeat the enemy.

The army that can achieve this level of security has already won even before joining the battle. Sun Tzu stated, "Thus a victorious army wins its victories before seeking battle."[21]

The most valuable armor soldiers can wear is the unshakable conviction that their commander has trained, equipped, and positioned them so mightily that victory is inevitable. These three facets of security were summed up by Sun Tzu when he said, "It is a doctrine of war not to assume the enemy will not come, but rather to rely on one's readiness to meet him; not to presume that he will not attack, but rather to make one's self invincible."[22]

Invincibility, then, is the supernatural original of the principle of security. And just as high as the heavens are above the Earth so is the secret of invincibility above human security. Here are its three facets:

1. *Our intelligence can allow us to outwit Satan and detect his attacks.* Our sources of information are astonishing. To begin with, the Word of God lays Satan bare. He is not all powerful. Ephesians 6:11 says, "Put on the whole armor of God, that you may be able to stand against the wiles of the devil." We are told here to be aware of Satan's wiles, not his power.

As our wisdom increases, he is gradually deteriorating: "However, we speak wisdom among those who are mature, yet not the wisdom of this age, nor of the rulers of this age, who are coming to nothing . . ." [I Corinthians 2:6]. He can be manipulated into gigantic blunders, such as when He crucified Christ. He cannot decode our wisdom because God has hidden it! "But we speak the wisdom of God in a mystery, the hidden wisdom which God ordained before the ages for our glory, which none of the rulers of this age knew; for had they known, they would not have crucified the Lord of glory" [I Corinthians 2:7-8].

Not only this but the Holy Spirit will tell us Lucifer's plans! Look at this example of intelligence:

"Now the king of Syria was making war against Israel; and he consulted with his servants, saying, 'My camp will be in such and such a place.' And the man of God sent to the king of Israel, saying, 'Beware that you do not pass this place, for the Syrians are coming down there.' Then the king of Israel sent someone to the place of which the man of God had told him. Thus he warned him, and he was watchful there, not just once or twice. Therefore the heart of the king of Syria was greatly troubled by this thing; and he called his servants and said to them, 'Will you not show me which of us is for the king of Israel?' And one of his servants said, 'None, my lord, O king; but Elisha, the prophet who is in

Israel, tells the king of Israel the words that you speak in your bedroom" [II Kings 6:8-12].

If God supernaturally helped a prophet know the plans of an enemy king, how much more will He help us against Satan! If necessary, God will carry one of His own to the very throne room of Satan to snatch his secrets.

2. *Supernatural Fortification.* Let me repeat Jesus's words in John 14:30: "I will no longer talk much with you, for the ruler of this world is coming, and he has nothing in Me." The message here is sobering. If Jesus had to implement security measures, then how much more we must close up breaches in our defense.

Armies must be aware of spies, but we must watch for an even more sinister and subtle traitor—our own flesh. Our carnal nature would gladly team up with the Evil One. Conquering this inner enemy is greater than any outward victory. "He who is slow to anger is better than the mighty, and he who rules his spirit than he who takes a city" [Proverbs 16:32].

We must treat our flesh as an even greater enemy than Satan because it can fool us from within and it is ever clawing to get its way!

Jonathan Edwards said, "A true saint is suspicious of nothing more than his own heart." The true warrior will be merciless to their carnal impulses and put armor over a weakness instantly. It is fortunate for us that so excellent a provision has been made for us. Paul promised, ". . . walk in the Spirit, and you will not fulfill the lusts of the flesh" [Galatians 5:16].

3. *Our Final Stand.* The Bible says, "We are more than conquerors through Him who loved us" [Romans 8:37].

The God-warrior's stand is clear:
I cannot be defeated!
My enemy cannot win!

Beyond any human general, our Mighty God can endow us with the conviction of certain victory and the irresistible will to attack. By putting on all six pieces of the armor of God, you are put beyond the possibility of defeat!

But what really is the armor of God? It is Christ Himself! He is our invincibility. Romans 13:14 tells us to ". . . put on the Lord Jesus Christ and make no provision for the flesh, to fulfil its lusts," because:

He is the Truth our waist is girded with:
"Jesus said to him. 'I am the way, the truth, and the life. No one comes to the Father except through Me'" [John 14:6].

He is the Breastplate of Righteousness:
"But of Him who are in Christ Jesus, who became for us wisdom from God—and righteousness and sanctification and redemption—" [I Corinthians 1:31].

He is the Preparation of the Gospel:
"How beautiful upon the mountains are the feet of him who brings good news, who proclaims peace, who brings glad tidings of good things, who proclaims salvation who says to Zion, 'Your God reigns!'" [Isaiah 52:7].

He is the Shield of Faith:
". . . looking unto Jesus, the author and finisher of our faith, who for the joy that was set before Him endured the cross, despising the shame, and has sat down at the right hand of the throne of God" [Hebrews 12:2].

He is the Helmet of Salvation:
"And she will bring forth a son, and you shall call His name Jesus, for He will save His people from their sins" [Matthew 1:21].

He is the Sword of the Spirit, the Word of God:
"In the beginning was the Word, and the Word was with God, and the Word was God" [John 1:1].

Put on all the armor! Make Satan pay dearly every time He attacks you. Do not act relieved that you survived the storm! Your work begins once the assault is over. Take note of what you were doing right before Satan pounced on you. Go back and do it more and more and more until Lucifer sees how disastrous it is to attack you because you are now the living, breathing embodiment of Him who, in Revelation 6:2, rode forth "conquering and to conquer!"

— Martin

The Secret of the Lord

Dear Warrior,

I call our next principle *The Secret of the Lord*.

In each generation God creates a mysterious trigger that, once pulled, blasts a hole in the very core of the Evil One's activity. What is so wonderful is how utterly undetectable it is to the Enemy until it is too late.

You may be wondering why I insist on connecting a principle of war to each of *the twelve secrets*. Let me explain by taking you back to when war was created.

Satan lusted after God's beauty, plundered Adam's royalty, pilfered Earth's glory, and thought He had stopped Jehovah's plan. By his actions, he declared war on God. Since war had never been seen before, where do you suppose Lucifer learned to wage war? By doing what he had always done—watching God and trying to imitate him.

Martin Luther said, "For where God built a church, there the Devil would also build a chapel . . . as the Most Holiest was dark, and had no light, even so and after the same manner did they [pagans] make their shrines dark where the Devil made answer. Thus is the Devil ever God's ape."[23]

God activated his attack strategies when he pronounced judgment on the Devil. God's campaign was to rescue Man and destroy evil. Therefore, His plan, of necessity, was complex and long-range.

The principles of war were created by "God's ape" as he tried to copy the very things he saw Jehovah doing. This brought judgment upon Satan. Satan's goal was to make war physical. He provoked Cain to murder his brother Abel. Bloodshed was born and the blood has never stopped flowing. Physical war gave Satan his greatest means of filling Hell. This is why he teaches Man war and foments as much conflict as possible.

The twelve secrets, then, are God's original truths that have been counterfeited by Satan. They are the expedients that God created to ultimately eradicate evil. This is why I am so adamant that we obey them and make ourselves accessible to the Lord's mighty power to attack the invisible and prevent war from turning physical.

Now let us study the principle of war that 'apes" *the secret of the Lord*. It is called *surprise.*

The element of surprise gives the aggressors a multi-faceted advantage. They choose where, when, and how they will attack. If their adversary is caught totally unaware, it can instantly break the morale and cause irreparable confusion.

The element of surprise can only affect your enemy in three instances: in relationship to time, place, and method. But two more conditions must exist before you can plan a surprise attack. First, you must be clearly *aware* of the condition of your enemy and his intentions, and secondly, he must be totally *unaware* of your conditions and intentions.

Security must be achieved before a surprise attack can even be considered. The troops must be disciplined and finely tuned for war. Von Clausewitz said, "Surprise will never be achieved under lax conditions and conduct."[24]

If I am a good general, my real goal is to take the enemy by complete surprise. Here then are the three components of complete surprise:

1. *Choosing my place of surprise.* My spies

have uncovered a weak point, but can my army mobilize to this point? Again, Von Clausewitz said, "The two factors that produce surprise are secrecy and speed."[25] The location you select blends these factors. You can get there quickly, rested, and undetected.

2. *Deciding the time of my attack.* Again, I must pit my strength against the enemy's weakness. My informants have given me a profile of my opponent's day to day operations. I choose my moment of attack carefully. It may be during a meal or while they sleep, or as Sun Tzu said, "During the early morning spirits are keen, during the day they flag, and in the evening thoughts turn toward home. And therefore those skilled in war avoid the enemy when his spirit is keen and attack him when it is sluggish and his soldiers homesick."[26] But I must also know what my troops' temperament is and when they will be able to give me their best fighting.

3. *Choosing my tactic of surprise.* Surprise attacks are excellent opportunities to display a new weapon or a novel method of attack. My prey is devastated not only by having no warning, but by not knowing what it is that they are up against.

If I have put all three of these factors in place

and I can be certain that my adversary does not know what they are, then I can anticipate a stunning victory.

Sun Tzu said, "Strike the enemy as swiftly as a falcon strikes its target. It surely breaks the back of its prey for the reason that it awaits for the right moment to attack."[27]

True surprise has eluded armies for millenniums. As a tactic, surprise is ever present, but hardly perfect. It has failed as often as it has worked, and when it fails, the losses are huge. Von Clausewitz says, "But while the wish to achieve surprise is common, and indeed indispensable, and while it is true that it will never be completely ineffective, it is equally true that by its very nature surprise can rarely be outstandingly successful. It would be a mistake, therefore, to regard surprise as a key element in success in war."[28]

There is no record of a perfect surprise in warfare, except maybe one—Gideon! But that is because it was not mere human surprise. It was *the secret of the Lord*!

As Gideon hid in the wine vat, terrified of the Midianites, an angel appeared and tried to keep a straight face as he proclaimed Gideon a "mighty man of valor" [Judges 6:12]. Gideon was so far from greatness, that no demon was assigned to watch him. The mystery of Jehovah had begun! The world's most unlikeliest general began to build the unlikeliest army. At its peak, Gideon's army was outnumbered but then God began downsizing it.

And the Lord said to Gideon, "The people who are with you are too many for Me to give the Midianites into their hands, lest Israel claim glory for itself against Me, saying, 'My own hand has saved me'" [Judges 7:2]. Finally, the number that would bring perfect surprise was reached. "Then the Lord said to Gideon, 'By the three hundred men who lapped I will save you, and deliver the Midianites into your hand. Let all the other people go, every man to his place'" [Judges 7:7].

God had designed the three imperatives for total surprise. He had chosen the place, the time, and the method. When all of these soldiers were in their proper position, they launched the most original offensive strike of war in history.

"Then the three companies blew the trumpets and broke the pitchers—they held the torches in their left hands for blowing—and they cried, 'The sword of the Lord and of Gideon!' And every man stood in his place all around the camp; and the whole army ran and cried out and fled. When the three hundred blew the trumpets, the Lord set every man's sword against his companion throughout the whole camp" [Judges 7:20-22a]. The result for Gideon and his army was unqualified victory. The true nature of the *secret of the Lord* is that no one can be credited for its success but God. And God is always successful at surprise for two reasons:

(1) *He cannot be surprised.*
(2) *He can surprise anybody.*

But the ultimate expression of the *secret of the Lord* comes in the birth, life, and resurrection of Jesus.

To begin with Jehovah moved prophets to prophesy concerning the Messiah. These prophesies, though completely accurate, set a cosmic trap for Beelzebub by playing to his arrogance.

Look at Isaiah 9:6-7a: "For unto us a Child is born, unto us a Son is given; and the government will be upon His shoulders. And His name will be called Wonderful, Counselor, Mighty God, Everlasting Father, Prince of Peace. Of the increase of His government and peace there will be no end." Here is the portrait of a Mighty Ruler whose kingdom will not cease to expand. Satan's response is to position his forces to look for a Child who will be born to a prominent and powerful family, probably in a lavish palace. As soon as he is settled upon this tactic, Micah prophesies something completely different:

"But you, Bethlehem Ephrathah, though you are little among the thousands of Judah, yet out of you shall come forth to Me the One to be Ruler in Israel, whose goings forth are from of old, from everlasting" [Micah 5:2]. God designed this paradox so that Satan would be confused by his own evil. Satan could not figure out where to concentrate his forces. Even with the clue about the poor village of Bethlehem, the Devil would be fooled because Joseph and Mary were in another poor village, Nazareth. They would not arrive in Bethlehem until the last moment because of a census ordered by Caesar Augustus that was, in fact, manipulated by the Almighty.

God had established the *where* and the *when*, but the crowning achievement was the *how*. The world had never before imagined a virgin birth, let alone expected one. The manger was a tactically perfect surprise.

God is building another surprise. Its fulfillment looks totally unpromising. "And this gospel of the kingdom will be preached in all the world as a witness to all the nations, and then the end will come" [Matthew 24:14]. At this moment there are a host of unlikely heroes secretly being built up into a global assault force. Meanwhile, world events are folding into the positions that will best facilitate a worldwide harvest. *You* must break yourself free from the deception of seeking a human security. Instead you should pursue *the secret of the Lord.*

A key verse is Psalm 25:24 where it says, "The secret of the Lord is with those who fear Him, and He will show them His covenant." Those who are more in awe of the Lord than current events have a special power. "Do not say, 'A conspiracy,' concerning all that this people call a conspiracy, nor be afraid of their threats, nor be troubled. The Lord of hosts, Him you shall hallow; let Him be your fear. And let Him be your dread. He will be as a sanctuary . . ." [Isaiah 8:12-14a].

There is a part of this mystery that belongs to you. God will become your sanctuary in an insane world. God will show you his secret and his covenant. I must ask you this question, "What are you planning to do with your future?" I assure you that if it can be done by your own talent and resources then it is probably not of the Lord. His plan for you is something so big that you cannot do it without Him. Your aspirations should have the fragrance of the impossible. But this is not a call to a rash and reckless life. We need not even invent a strategy. The surprise is in progress. We merely need to find where we fit.

Yet again Satan is spread thin by prophetic mysteries. How depressed it makes him to realize that "Gideons" just keep appearing at needed times of worldwide darkness. Still, the crowning act of surprise will be in the skies. It is one shrouded in such mystery that no man knows the

hour or the day. This will not be 300 men blowing trumpets and shouting, but the trump of
God and the roar of Jesus! A lightening bolt will
cross the entire sky. The heavens will roll up like
a scroll and all evil will collapse at once!

— Martin

The Unity of the Spirit

Dear Warrior,

I wish you could have seen what a motley crew we were, what a bizarre cross-section of leaders! From all over China we were summoned to a central location by our denomination. The reason? A young church-growth expert had been sent over from one of our American schools of theology. He was going to help us.

My sons bitterly protested going to the meeting. They had faced snake-infested rivers, communist persecution, and hordes of demonized villagers. This seminar, however, was the supreme torture. "Why," they complained "should we listen to a *hot shot* whose only weapon is a frayed library card and whose theories could only live in a theological incubator?"

I told them that they must go because there was a higher purpose for our attendance. Our movement at home was deeply divided, and this division had spread to China. Many leaders refused to work together, and no matter how righteous their reasons, the final damage was seen in a lack of soul winning.

My purpose in attending was to try to heal rifts and confront the real issues as I saw them. My hope was that a great united force could be created to harvest the Chinese.

As we entered the meeting hall, I saw enemies of our work. The air was thick with the fog of politics, but I also saw mighty men and women of God. I hoped that these great people of God would stand with me as I gave my plea. I was committed to share my heart even if it meant sitting through a convoluted pep talk.

What I was not prepared for was the marketing message that was inflicted upon us by this young man from America. He preached in the full fever of his own self-importance.

Early in my ministry I was sternly warned of a pulpit disease called *ignorance on fire*. Here it was before me in full conflagration. Some way, though I cannot tell you how, he had melded concepts of pop psychology, new age nonsense, and a hamburger sales philosophy into a formula for reaching the Chinese. The closest he came to relating to China was in his creation of a phenomenon that *sounded* Chinese. It was *Confusionism*!

In his own style, the speaker tried to explain spiritual warfare. There were regional devils, he surmised, that were called territorial spirits. All we needed was a spiritual map and official name for these devils. He showed us a cute ceremony. We could scold these beings by name, they would leave, and instant breakthrough would ensue.

I looked around the room and there, sprinkled among the crowd, were true warriors of God. How could this consultant appreciate the fact that he was talking to mighty apostles who had carved churches out of the granite of communist China, deposed demons en masse, and had even raised the dead?

I prayed vehemently for a chance to speak. God answered my prayer in the strangest way. He used the arrogance of the speaker. As hard as I tried, I could not mask my feelings about his speech. Suddenly he asked me what I thought. I detected that he did this in order to cause a confrontation between his ideas and mine. It was as though he wanted to verify the superiority of his theories by exposing mine.

I assumed that he saw me as one who represented the "old way of doing things." He, of course, was representing the "new way." He wanted to prove that my position was antiquated and that our denomination could be improved by humanism. There was no small commotion when I asked for and received permission to answer him from the pulpit.

When everyone got quiet I told the young man that I thought he was very sincere but, of course, wrong. I directed the audience's attention to Acts, Chapter 8, and showed them Philip preaching in the city of Samaria which was dominated by the occult. "Then Philip went down to the city of Samaria and preached Christ to them. And the multitudes with one accord heeded the things spoken by Philip, hearing and seeing the miracles which he did. For unclean spirits, crying with a loud voice, came out of many who were possessed; and many who were paralyzed and lame were healed. And there was great joy in that city" [Acts 8:5-8]. Philip received no name for these devils nor did he need a spiritual road map. He knew that the way you get devils out is by bringing in the mighty gospel!

I told him that the only part of his presentation that I agreed with was the existence of territorial spirits. "There are ruling spirits that control specific regions, but they are not demons," I explained. "They are leaders right here in this room, who have, and I say this with a broken heart, divided up the work of God. Instead of being a cooperative force that pulls together talent and manpower, there is isolation, possessiveness and competition. The tragedy is that there are more than enough talent, prayer power, and resources present here to overwhelm any power of darkness in China. Our problem is not on the outside of us, but within us. A God-given unity and a combined witness would automatically loosen the grip of Satan."

After I finished speaking, the Spirit of God fell. Soon leaders began to shake violently and sob uncontrollably. A great miracle that would bring untold life to China was born that day. What was that great miracle? *The secret of the unity of the Spirit.*

This gift of God crumbles walls between people and sets hearts aflame so that they are utterly available to God. This builds a tidal wave against the devil's targets.

Once again, to fully grasp its scope and breadth, we must study its physical counterpart. It is the principle of war known as *cooperation.*

First and foremost, the principle of cooperation is an attitude. It is the ability to willingly marshall forces that are under separate command and bring them under the authority of the Commander-in-Chief. Cooperation is a spirit that says, in effect, whatever it takes to win we shall do. Each separate unit is obsessed with adding whatever talent they have to the cause of victory in whatever way they are asked to do it.

Sun Tzu said, "Now the troops of those adept in war are used like the 'Simultaneously

Responding' snake of Mount Ch'ang. When struck on the head its tail attacks; when struck on the tail, its head attacks, when struck in the centre both head and tail attack. Should one ask: 'Can troops be made capable of such instantaneous co-ordination?' I reply: 'They can.' For, although the men of Wu and Yüeh mutually hate one another, if together in a boat tossed by the wind, they would co-operate as the right hand does with the left."[29]

Without cooperation, troops cannot concentrate at the decisive point. There have been numerous times in the history of war, that even though an attack force was clearly superior, it lost. For, even when an army possesses superior intelligence and arms, lack of cooperation neutralizes their advantage.

Cooperation, in a military campaign, is hard to achieve. Here are the classic reasons why:

1. *Unit pride.*

In the early stages of training, a big emphasis is put into pride and loyalty to your unit. This builds a strong loyalty as well to the unit leader. The problem comes when the training is finished, and these men must now advance as a unit and combine with the other elements of the army. They must now transfer their loyalty from their leader to the battle commander.

Their pride is deep. They have been drilled over and over that their own unit is the best. They are confident that they can "do it alone" and become belligerent to the other parts of the fighting force.

2. *The authority is too detached.*

Fighting battalions that have been used to very close and immediate superiors now find it difficult to heed the commands of authority that are distant and inaccessible.

3. *Disloyalty to the Commander-in-Chief.*

Whoever has created the objective and has been given absolute authority over the battle plan must command the entire operation, as well as each and every branch of the fighting machine. When subordinate leaders have enthralled their soldiers with how much better they could run the war, there is a disloyalty that ruins cooperation. Such a condition will cause disaster. Sun Tzu said, "When senior officers are angry and insubordinate, and on encountering the enemy rush into battle with no understanding of the feasibility of engaging and without awaiting orders from the commander, the army is in a state of collapse."[30]

The Commander-in-Chief knows why certain plans have been made; that wisdom is not al-

ways available to subordinate leaders. Therefore, loyalty to the Commander-in-Chief is the
essence of cooperation.

These same three problems plague the Christian movement:

1. *Unit pride.*

A church or denomination emulates unit
pride when they believe that they have more
truth and are so right that they dare not pollute
themselves by cooperating with the rest of the
Body of Christ. They conjure up a host of "holy
reasons" why they cannot get involved in a citywide effort to win souls. In their blindness, they
will *defend to the death* a doctrinal technicality
while violating the undeniable truths of God's
love and the great commission. How well did
Jesus describe them in Matthew 23:24: "Blind
guides, who strain out a gnat and swallow a
camel!"

2. *Detached authority.*

If Christian leaders are too overbearing and
dictatorial, they can dull the hearing of disciples
who can then barely hear Jesus. Small wonder,
then, that the Lord's authority over them feels
distant and detached.

The Bible says in I Peter 5:2-4: "Shepherd the
flock of God which is among you, serving as
overseers, not by compulsion but willingly, not

for dishonest gain but eagerly; nor as being lords over those entrusted to you, but being examples to the flock; and when the Chief Shepherd appears, you will receive the crown of glory that does not fade away." Every pastor knows that they will surrender the sheep to the Lord on "that day." But the true pastor knows that he must surrender the sheep *every* day.

When a battalion leader acts independently of his commander, he might use the excuse that the leader is too detached or that it would be too ponderous to go through proper channels when snap decisions must be made. This excuse, however, will not spare him from severe discipline.

How much more guilty, then, are we as leaders when we act independently from our Commander Jesus Christ! We can be instantly in His presence, and He is never detached: "For lo, I am with you to the end of the age" [Matthew 28:20].

When the Chief Shepherd summons the sheep for a citywide harvest, the pastor must recognize the "up close" authority of the Holy Spirit to do so!

3. *Disloyalty to the Commander-in-Chief.*
Let's face it. The true source of division is almost always that the heart is not right with Christ. If I am right with Jesus, it follows that

I cannot be divided against another who is likewise in harmony with the Lord.

There is always someone who will race to take
the moral high ground and make all sorts of fervent excuses for causing division. The Biblical
grounds for such dissecting of the church, however, are extremely limited. Most of what we see
is plain disloyalty to the Lord as the Head of the
Church. To be sure, there are a lot of righteous
words spouted, but few of them are in deliberate
prayer. Few people ever asked the Commander-
in-Chief what they should do. If they did, he
would almost surely recite the words of Paul in
Ephesians 4:3 instructing them to ". . . keep the
unity of the Spirit in the bond of peace." Here
are the elements of *the unity of the Spirit:*

It is vertical before it is horizontal.

By this I mean that it is futile to "get everyone together and reconcile." This comes only after individual repentance before God. When I
am in vertical unity with the Spirit, then I can
reach out horizontally to my brother who is also
Spirit-led.

The supreme commandment is: "You shall
love the Lord your God with all your heart,
with all your soul, and with all your mind, this
is the first and great commandment. And the
second is like it: You shall love your neighbor as

yourself" [Matthew 22:37-38]. Your love must be connected *upward*—"love God"—before it can go *outward*—"your neighbor as yourself."

Many have sought to enforce unity in the hopes that it would cause an outpouring. But it is the vertical repentance that brings the Holy Spirit who then brings unity.

In the upper room the disciples were not praying for unity. They got unity because they were repenting and asking for the Holy Spirit.

It is supernatural agreement!

"Again I say to you that if two of you agree on earth concerning anything that they ask, it will be done for them by My Father in heaven. For where two or three are gathered together in My name, I am there in the midst of them" [Matthew 18:19-20].

As touching *anything?* Does it really mean *anything?* The fact that it does should ignite us to seek the gift of supernatural agreement with every atom of our being.

All things are possible because we have repented and let Jesus be the "I am in the midst" of us. Having tossed aside our inferior purposes like defective toys, we are utterly available to substitute those things that God keeps ready for those who love him for our puny ideas [I Corinthians 2:9]. Pray mighty prayers, prayers that are not only out of our reach but have not even entered our minds!

Agreement is such a powerful force that God said of the men of the Tower of Babel: ". . . Indeed the people are one and they all have one language, and this is what they begin to do; now nothing that they propose to do will be withheld from them. Come, let Us go down and there confuse their language, that they may not understand one another's speech" [Genesis 11:6-7]. Agreement is so powerful that when God saw men achieve it without Him, He knew that they would use it to create an awesome perversion. God had to intervene!

Imagine, then, the creative force of God's Christian warriors achieving agreement by the power of the Holy Spirit. The world has yet to see the astonishing exploits they would do.

Unity in the Holy Spirit is *koinonia*. *"A new commandment I give to you, that you love one another; as I have loved you, that you also love one another. By this all will know that you are My disciples, if you have love for one another"* [John 13:34-35].

The word *koinonia* did not exist until there were Christians. The Greeks saw the life-infusing effect that Christians had on each other. They had many words for fellowship but nothing to describe family that had such joy and love and that experienced such intense refreshment from each other. So, they called it koinonia.

One night a Roman guard stood watch outside a nobleman's mansion during a great feast. There was abundance, laughter, and revelry inside. It represented all that this soldier was aspiring to gain in his lifetime. All at once he heard faint singing coming up from the gutter. It was the Christians in the catacombs underneath the streets of Rome. Here the sound of God's people enjoying fellowship and worship was colliding with the sound of pleasure and ease above.

He heard both sounds for hours and his heart began to warm. It was a miracle that defies description. The worship of the saints had drained the attraction of the feast in this man's heart. His tears flowed, and he made his choice. He walked over and lifted the grate that the covered the gutter and climbed down to join the family of God.

—Martin

Communion

Dear Warrior,

A weak prayer life will make you feel more guilty than anything else. One reason for this is that you know how crucial prayer is to everything you do. As believers, we are continually drilled about the preeminence of prayer.

Let us examine a typical morning in your life. You wake up frantically. You are in a race. The slightest misstep will put you perilously behind schedule. As you are about to blast out the door, you feel an overwhelming shame that you have not prayed. *Is this Holy Ghost conviction?* Most likely it is a very subtle, but debilitating, assault from Satan.

This attack is comparable to a common mistake made by moms and dads. Their child has just behaved foolishly. Out of exasperation, one of the parents snaps at the youngster, "How could you do something so stupid!" This comment was meant to teach the child to think before they act. The actual result, however, is just the opposite. The child feels embarrassed, ashamed, and yes, stupid.

If all this damage to the child's esteem was done by accident, imagine, then, what shame can be like in the hands of Satan who is purposing to destroy you! The voice that is assaulting you as you walk out the door in the morning is not trying to get you to pray, but to feel ashamed; so ashamed, in fact, that you won't enter God's presence, and you will postpone prayer indefinitely.

Hear me, Warrior: Satan can be more dangerous barking at us to do what is right than he can when he tempts us to do what is wrong.

Of course, the answer is not to feel exempt from prayer just because we have uncovered his devilish plot! No, it is just the opposite. We are now alert to the fact that Lucifer is trying to destroy our prayer life.

The key is to distinguish between the voice of the Holy Spirit and the voice of the Evil One. There is a classic difference between the two. The Holy Spirit provokes prayer from within, not with an angry tone, but by warming the heart and making us lonesome to be with God.

Jesus called the Holy Spirit "The Helper." Beware, then, of inner urgings that seem right but don't help you. It is the impulse of the Spirit of the Lord to "fan into flame" any spark of God that is within us.

There are three great misunderstandings about prayer, and three greater answers to those misunderstandings. They are:

1. *I have gone a long time without prayer. I dread the anger of the Lord I will feel once I finally do pray.*

The most amazing experience of your life will be when you see how glad God is to hear from you. There will be no mention of the separation, except that He missed you.

2. *I must wait until I have time to pray for hours.*

Some may deem my next remark as unspiritual. It is not as important to the Holy Spirit how long you pray as how often you pray. You can begin with five minutes a day. Do not be afraid to start small.

3. *I truly have no time to pray.*

While some would never believe that remark, for many people, it is totally true. They need to see the power prayer has to create time. It liberates time. Prayer replaces all the time it uses and gives back so much more. Here is how: (a) There are many things you do that take much longer than they should because you are not refreshed, alert, and strong, and (b) there are many thieves of your time you cannot see except through the eye of prayer.

When you face the fear of interrupting your routine and steal off to meet the Master, a divine order will dispose the chaos in your life. You will be free at last. Prayer will then become addictive! *Soon you will be ready to make the quantum leap from a prayer life to a life of prayer.*

The Old Testament showcases men and women who were granted extraordinary intimacy with God. The Bible says that Moses knew God face to face: "So the Lord spoke to Moses face to face, as a man speaks to his friend" [Exodus 33:11]. This strange and wondrous friendship grew to harness history itself! Daniel 11:32 says: "But the people who know their God will be strong and carry out great exploits." Daniel knew that at the *end of the age* there would be people who would experience a rare intimacy with God and would do greater things than had ever been done before.

This intimacy is provided by the righteousness of Jesus Christ and is credited to every believer by the faith that Jesus imparts. So righteous is this impartation that we are granted audience at the throne of God which exceeds what God gave to Moses!

Intimacy is what your next secret is about. It is called *communion with God*. This celestial secret has an earthly counterpart. In this case, it is a principle of war known as "lines of communication."

Von Clausewitz described lines of communication this way: "They link the army to its base and must be considered as its arteries. The roads are in constant use for all sorts of deliveries, for ammunition convoys, detachments moving back and forth, mail carriers and couriers, hospitals and depots, reserve munitions, and administrative personnel. All this together is vital to the army."[31]

Lines of communication, then, are all the routes, whether by land, air, or sea that connect an operating military force with its base of operation. All of their supplies and reinforcements move along these routes.

Sun Tzu called lines of communication *doctrine* when he said, "By doctrine I mean organization, control, assignment of appropriate ranks to officers, regulation of supply routes, and the provision of principal items used by the army"[32]

Napoleon said, "An army marches on its stomach." How well he knew that! Twice he lost major wars because his supply lines were disrupted. On those occasions he had violated his lines of communication.

There are two precautions a general must keep in mind in regards to lines of communication:

1. He must secure his lines of communication or the enemy will cut off his supply routes.
2. He must not outrun his own supply line. Even if he wins a battle, his resources will be depleted and will likely allow his opponent to regroup in a counteroffensive.

Effective supply lines give an army significant advantages: (a) they allow it to continuously advance, and (b) the army arrives at its goal with strength and reserve. This guarantees victory because it is a double dose of morale for the soldiers. They feel excited because they are *on the move,* taking enemy territory, and they are not cold, hungry, or low on ammunition.

Many immediate comparisons can be made to God's army.

1. *We must not allow our supply line to be disrupted.* Our Supplier is the Holy Spirit. We remain constant in prayer because the warfare is intense and dependence on God is more essential than ever before.

2. *We must not outrun our supply line.* This is when we become overextended. Paul said he

avoided this in II Corinthians 10:13-14: "We, however, will not boast beyond measure, but within the limits of the sphere which God appointed us—a sphere which especially includes you. For we are not overextending ourselves (as though our authority did not extend to you), for it was to you that we came with the gospel of Christ."

In Psalms 106:13 it says, "They soon forgot His works; they did not wait for His counsel."

Natural armies experience overextension because their supply lines *cannot* keep up, but with Christians, it may be because God *will not* keep up.

The provision of the Lord is for the vision of the Lord. There is no room for human counsel or pet projects on the front line of our war! Our program must be for the pleasure of the Lord.

Jesus did what He saw His father doing. ". . . My Father has been working until now, and I have been working" [John 5:17]. His communion with His Father was His line of communication! This was His supply line to keep moving and taking new ground. But there is still more! Communion has three very amazing features.

1. *Communion is Intimacy.*
"And he gave unto Moses, when he had made

an end of communing with him upon mount Sinai, two tables of testimony, tables of stone, written with the finger of God" [Exodus 31:18 KJV].

Before Moses could receive the commandments, God insisted on communion! It is hard to relate this mystery. What did Moses and God do for those forty days? The answer strikes at the heart of why God made us — *to commune with Him*. Just as God had intimate walks with Adam in the cool of the evening, now Moses experienced that same intimacy.

The demands of the Lord grow out of a relationship. Until we behold the wonder of His glory, love, and goodness, we cannot see the power and rightness of God's principles.

David said, "Open my eyes, that I may see wondrous things from your law" [Psalm 119:18]. Religion is, in essence, rules without relationship.

Ask a child the difference it makes in their ability to learn when they love their teacher!

But even Moses could not enjoy *full* intimacy with God. Fullness of intimacy came when Jesus offered it to the disciples. This kind of intimacy had not been seen since the Garden of Eden. "No longer do I call you servants, for a servant does not know what his master is doing; but I have called you friends, for all things that I heard from My Father I have made known to you" [John 15:15].

Everything we do for God must be the secondary result of an eternal bond. The next verse is a prelude to what grows out of communion: "You did not choose Me, but I chose you and appointed you that you should go and bear fruit, and that your fruit should remain, that whatever you ask the Father in My name He may give you" [John 15:16].

2. *Communion is Provision.* Anyone who has walked with the Lord in intimacy will tell you that God makes big demands and gives big rewards. There is an unalterable fact about our Master: He provides more than enough for His purposes.

Earthly armies have to wait for supplies. We don't, because our provision from God is instant, open, and abundant.

We need never let up our penetration of evil territory to wait for ammunition or supplies. The promise of never having to let up on the attack is seen in II Corinthians 9:8: "And God is able to make all grace abound toward you, that you, always having all sufficiency in all things, may have an abundance for every good work."

Remember, I told you how high it makes the morale of soldiers climb when they penetrate enemy ground and are well equipped. Our morale can be infinitely greater!

First, we plunge into an eternal love bond

with Jehovah. This gives us unbroken intimacy. Next, we go out freely to press the assault, knowing clearly that our great cause is born of God. Our supply line will continually overtake us!

Here is Paul's proclamation of communion provision: ". . . that He would grant you, according to the riches of His glory, to be strengthened with might through His Spirit in the inner man, that Christ may dwell in your hearts through faith; that you, being rooted and grounded in love, may be able to comprehend with all the saints what is the width and length and depth and height—to know the love of Christ which passes knowledge; that you may be filled with all the fullness of God" [Ephesians 3:16-19].

3. Communion is Heaven's Prayer.

Once in a great while someone will pray a fervent and availing prayer. In fact, this prayer is so effectual that it crosses the veil and permits the petitioner to peer into heaven. The person praying catches a glimpse of Jesus in intercession. This is both glorious and painful at the same time. The petitioner rejoices at the revelation, but is cut to the heart by how much higher and purer the intercession of Jesus is than his own.

Our best prayer can still be cluttered with self-interest. Too often we are jockeying in prayer to find a short-cut out of failure. Then there are the prayers asking for relief from crisis without appreciating the deeper intention of the trial.

Daniel could have easily justified a panic prayer time. He had been kidnapped and taken to Babylon. Daniel's future plans had been cut off. He prayed and looked into heaven. There he saw and understood that God had business for him in Babylon. Daniel replaced his own prayer with heaven's prayer.

For some reason we cannot accept the fact that God will not act on Man's behalf outside of prayer. There is a continual, divine quest for someone to stand in the gap, and with an all consuming passion, pray the prayers that have been orphaned by our neglect. It is as if Jesus is saying, "Here, take this prayer and nurture it to fruition."

Every great revival can be traced to an astonishing gushing out of unselfish prayer, prayer that found its beginning in God.

Communion can give this prayer to you! You can be emptied of all your own affairs and pray in supernatural conformity with the deepest yearnings of Jesus. Arthur Mathew described it as this: "It is the overflow of a heart that the Holy Spirit has rendered sensitive to spiritual issues in earthly situations poured out in a steady, uninhibited stream of undiluted longing."[33]

Now can you understand the kind of soldier these three elements would create? A warrior, who is eternally bonded in love with his God, marches forward, never letting up on the attack. He draws on a never-ending supply of all that he needs for victory. He prays down the very power of heaven without limitation because his heart reflects the passion of his God.

Tell me, then, can you imagine anything
that can terrify Satan more
than a warrior in communion with God?

—Martin

Dunamis

When you think of *dunamis* you probably picture the raw power of God. After all, the word dynamite comes from the word dunamis. But dunamis is not the raw power of God; that would be the steel punch discussed in Secret #3. Dunamis is a very specialized and unique expression of power, so unique in fact, that I do not want you to relate to it as "the next secret," but as something that permeates all the other secrets.

Before I define dunamis for you, I must show you, yet again, the physical principle of war that corresponds to dunamis. It is called *economy of force*.

Economy of force is defined as fighting efficiently. Simply stated, it is using your army and equipment skillfully, without waste, to bring the maximum force possible. Von Clausewitz described economy of force this way: ". . . always to make sure that all forces are involved—

always to ensure that no part of the whole force is idle. If a segment of one's force is located where it is not sufficiently busy with the enemy, or if troops are on the march—that is, idle—while the enemy is fighting, then these forces are being managed uneconomically."[34]

Economy of force is using the right weapon in the right way and at the right place. Economy of force is a discipline that helps you discover why your army is not effective and a gauge to see how well you are obeying the principles of war. Here are some common violations of economy of force as they occur in each principle of war:

The Objective:
The soldiers do not know why they are fighting. They fight sluggishly and inconsistently. They are confused in purpose and cannot act as a unit. War is extended unnecessarily and wastes lives and resources.

The Offensive:
The soldiers do not have the will to attack. They are on the battlefield but they don't fire their weapons. This literally happened on D-Day at Omaha Beach during World War II. "Only five infantry companies [on Omaha Beach, June 6, 1944] were tactically effective. In these companies, one-fifth of the men fired their

weapons during the day-long advance from the water's edge to the first row of villages—total of not more than 450 men firing consistently."[35] Had all of the men fired their weapons, the battle would have been decided quickly and with far less loss of life.

Concentration:
The army is gathered at non-decisive points. Barracks are fine for training, but warriors must be taken to the *front* to attack the enemy. If not, it is a total waste of resources.

Mobility:
The army is too slow to get to a decisive point which allows the enemy to arrive first. The slow battalion is always tired and in danger. Swiftness economizes every resource of an army, especially time.

Security:
Internal strife and division breaches security and prevents protection. Valuable resources meant for attack are used up in the camp, and delayed attacks deleteriously affect morale.

Surprise:
Muddled information eliminates the ability to prepare for a surprise attack. Again, delay damages you by letting the enemy "shape you"

so that no surprise is possible. They know where you are going and how big you are!

Cooperation:
Because branches of the fighting force won't work together, attacks lack momentum and magnitude. They extend battles by exposing soldiers to overwhelming forces. New weapons are not tried because of bias. Commanders, who are jealous of each other, won't try them. There is no massive, focused, versatile assault. Here is the ultimate abuse of resources!

Lines of Communication:
When the enemy cuts off the supply line, that causes the ultimate waste. Not only have resources been lost, they become reinforcements for the enemy.

Surely you can see how economy of force is central to victory in physical war. How much more, then, is dunamis a force for us to use against Lucifer.

We have wasted more resources than any army in history! Without a doubt, Satan has cherished our ignorance of effective and efficient warfare.

Dunamis is a creative force of undiluted effectiveness. Dunamis is a power that blends the wisdom of the Holy Spirit, the power of the resurrection, and the grace of God into a cunning for total victory—the dynamite of God that renders us effective.

Many around the world have known dunamis as the anointing, and it is clearly described in the words of Jesus in Luke 4:18-19: "The Spirit of the Lord is upon Me, because he has anointed me to preach the gospel to the poor; He has sent me to heal the brokenhearted, to proclaim liberty to the captives, and recovery of sight to the blind, to set at liberty those who are oppressed; to proclaim the acceptable year of the Lord."

Let's look at Gideon once again. This time notice the impulse of dunamis. From the moment that Gideon obeyed God in preparing an attack against the Midianites, dunamis guided him. How?

1. He cut out all activities that did not relate to the giant *why* of his life.
2. He reduced the army in number until only the conative core was left.
3. He blended tactics into a maximized whole. With divine skill, he orchestrated pitchers to break, trumpets to blast, and soldiers to shout the victory!

No human training could have given Gideon this talent. A brilliant military career could not endow an officer with Gideon's surgical accuracy of attack.

Noah was infused with skills that still give pause today. He built something that had never been seen before. He did not have the privilege granted to most inventors of starting with a prototype.

Have you ever heard of an invention where the first rendering worked perfectly? Never mind its mathematically perfect proportions or the miracle of the placement of the animals. What boggles the mind was the structural integrity of the ark. What Noah constructed withstood a global catastrophe with the most violent wind and waves ever known.

Summon today's most respected shipbuilders, arm them with leading edge computer technology, and they could not, in a thousand tries, create with gopher wood what one man did with his hands under the impulse of dunamis.

How many people today boast about the information age! Thousands of years before these roosters crowed, Solomon prayed for dunamis. Solomon asked for the gift to rule the people of God. Soon gracious words of insight flowed like a river. The world came to Jerusalem to drink deeply of his godly counsel.

Dunamis is available today in a form that is beyond the wonder of these Bible heroes. Let us turn to the moment when the Apostle Paul asked the Corinthians a burning question:

"Therefore if the whole church comes together in one place, and all speak with tongues, and there come in those who are uninformed or unbelievers, will they not say that you are out of your mind? But if all prophesy, and an unbeliever or an uninformed person comes in, he is convinced by all, he is convicted by all. And thus the secrets of his heart are revealed; and so, falling down on his face, he will worship God and report that God is truly among you" [I Corinthians 14:23-25]. Paul called the question.

He is asking, in effect, "What kind of gatherings do you want?" Gatherings where onlookers leave disgusted and thinking you are insane, or a manifestation of prophetic persuasiveness where onlookers collapse before the truth and admit the reality of God? Do we want selfish supernaturalism that gratifies our emotions, but totally confuses the outsider? It is dunamis that arms us with the skill to rightly express the miraculous gifts of God.

There is an impact that the Holy Spirit has designed, but we have allowed key violations of economy of force to give the Devil access to our effectiveness. Here is how:

1. Satan fights to separate key ingredients that together create an awesome impact. He wants dichotomy when there should be integrity. Here are examples of his favorite dichotomies:

To separate love and knowledge.
To separate miracles and order.
To separate joy and holiness.
To separate teaching and soul winning.

Lucifer poisons the church with pride so that factions become fiercely loyal to a single ingredient. These people refuse to appreciate their missing component. Satan works unceasingly to keep gifts and weapons separated when, in union, they would cause him great harm.

2. Satan has kept us concentrated at points that are not decisive. We are in church preaching the gospel to each other. Since we are not deployed to assault the Devil, we eventually attack one another.

Dunamis is skill on fire and wisdom at war. But it imparts so much more than this. It refuses to waste force and will send the church to centers of evil!

As I said earlier, leaders who are in denial invent pseudo-victories to busy the army of God and keep them in the barracks after their training is complete. Look around you. You will see churches and Christians organizations that are really good at one thing, but it doesn't matter. All of that talent is wasted if it is not connected to the gifts of other churches and is not expressed at decisive points.

Dunamis will not tolerate this condition for a single moment. It will marshall all of the detached units. It will blend all the weapons and will apply whatever pressure is needed to get the army to a meaningful target. But dunamis is still more . . .

Jesus said, "You shall receive δύναμις (dunamis) and be a witness" [Acts 1:8]. He is saying so much more than we know! A true witness is armed with skills to decode a culture and sense the vacuum of a generation. The person speaks the precise words in the precise way that renders the hearer defenseless before the love of God.

Luke 21:15 describes pure dunamis: "For I will give you a mouth and wisdom which all your adversaries will not be able to contradict or resist." Isaiah echoes this same gift: "The Lord God has given Me the tongue of the learned, that I should know how to speak a word in season to him who is weary. He awakens Me morning by morning. He awakens My ear to hear as the learned" [Isaiah 50:4].

Pentecost is misunderstood! We miss the true significance of that day! Yes, there was wind and fire and the wondrous arrival of the Holy Spirit, but above all, there was a witness! All *twelve secrets* came together in a pulverizing moment of impact that made Jerusalem ground zero for Satan. It was not just a matter that onlookers were stunned that the 120 could suddenly speak their languages; it was the irresistible power of what they were saying. It was a direct message from the heart of God to the now unprotected hearts of the people. Fifteen thousand people met the Master in a moment! This phenomenon is hated the most by Satan. It is the extreme antithesis of what he tries to do.

Just as war fills Hell,
so does dunamis populate Heaven
with a myriad of souls!

—Martin

Divine Dissatisfaction

Dear Warrior,

What in war could be easier than to chase a defeated foe? After all, you have won and your enemy has lost! The fact is that many wars have been won by retreating armies. The reasons are clear to an experienced general.

1. The enemy has an inherent speed advantage. They are running for their lives! The winning army, on the other hand, has the euphoria of victory and the relief of winning. The enemy is motivated to run while the victor is motivated to stop and rest, having found a precious moment of relief.

Von Clausewitz said, "Each of the thousands under his command needs food and rest, and longs for nothing so much as a few hours free of danger and fatigue. Very few men—and they are the exceptions—are able to follow and feel beyond the present moment."[36] Finding the will to chase is difficult indeed!

2. The enemy is falling back on their supply lines and can be restored. Meanwhile, the winning army is advancing away from their supplies and may be taken in a counterattack. Von Clausewitz said, "If the defeated troops are only a minor part of the enemy's forces and have other units to fall back on or can look to strong reinforcements to arrive, the victor may easily run the risk of losing his gains at any moment."[37]

Military minds have concluded that troops must be skilled in the principle of war called *pursuit*. It has three qualities:

1. Pursuit is a mental toughness that allows an army to disregard emotions and do what must be done even after they believe they have won.
2. Pursuit is swiftness that can outrun a retreating army and persevere for as long as it takes.
3. Pursuit means to avoid attacking what is in front of you. Instead you run alongside the enemy. You are racing them back to their supplies in order to overtake them and cut off their retreat. Von Clausewitz

said, "Finally, the third and most effective degree of pursuit takes the form of marching parallel with the enemy toward the immediate goal of his retreat."[38]

Sun Tzu said, "He fixes a date for rendezvous and after the troops have met, cuts off their return route just as if he were removing a ladder from beneath them."[39]

Pursuit is an inner determination to settle for nothing less than absolute victory. For troops to possess this quality, they are trained and drilled repeatedly. There must exist a profound reverence and trust for their general. This is because he necessarily presses them to extreme limits of body and mind. The general in pursuit is casting his men into unknown danger! The retreating forces may have set traps, blown up bridges, and destroyed roads. Multiple distractions will try to ruin the swift pace.

A good general will indelibly mark his men with the importance of pursuit. He will pound that urgency into them. *Breakthrough is not a victory; it is only a greater opportunity for victory.*

The good general will use his army's hatred of war as fuel to gain final victory. He will remind his men that if the retreaters get away, they will have to go through all of this again!

God endows his warriors with a much deeper

version of the principle of pursuit. I call this secret *divine dissatisfaction*.

Possibly the most divinely dissatisfied man in history was Moses. He never quit pursuing the glory of God. He also never quit in battle. Because he handled warfare so well, we will study a classic episode of his life. This encounter will reveal the three ways that Satan assaults our quest for final victory.

Satan attacks right after victory.

Moses faced this at a place called Rephidim. We read about it in Exodus 17.

The miracle of the water from the rock had just happened. Then Satan stirred up the Amalekites to steal the water.

Moses was not so satisfied with this miracle that he would let down his guard. He instantly ordered Joshua to get the army ready: "And Moses said to Joshua, 'Choose us some men and go out, fight with Amalek . . .'" [Exodus 17:9a].

The Devil throws distractions to slow your pursuit.

Moses was not fooled by the Evil One's frontal attack. In fact, he headed in the opposite direction. He was practicing pursuit. He ignored the battle in front of him and, instead, raced to cut off the enemy's supply.

The Amalekites were controlled by the

demonic, and Moses knew it! He looked for elevation to raise the rod of God over the battle. He took his stand in the heavenlies!

Amalek began to feel the sting of defeat. The raised rod of God disrupted the Amalekites!

Beelzebub flatters you with pride and reputation in an effort to destroy you with false satisfaction.

But then, Moses's arms tired and weakened. The battle ebbed and flowed as the rod rose and fell. Lucifer tried to make the effort seem futile, but Moses refused to quit.

Aaron and Hur sat Moses on a rock and upheld his arms. Moses would not let himself become a legend who needed no help. He freely accepted Aaron's and Hur's reinforcement. Amalek was defeated! Moses cut off their retreat!

The divinely dissatisfied one never totally rejoices in victory. This is not just because he suspects attack, but because he is simply hungry for more. This is not ingratitude, but an insatiable desire to glorify God. Not only does this kind of warrior refuse to "rest on his laurels," he buries them in the ground! To him, past achievement is a seed planted from which will grow a new exploit.

Satan wants to use your last victory against

you. He will try a *shock attack*, hoping that in your celebrating you will have let your guard down. He will try the paralyzing influence of reputation. He surrounds you with the "praises of men" so that your hunger and edge are dulled. You loosen your grip on excellence. Most of all, a victory-hungry warrior is not fooled into thinking that a miracle includes some big buffer of time against return fire.

Again, Moses did not try to analyze the theological implications of getting miracle water one moment and an assault the next. He was ready! Like Moses, we are not to attack the circumstance in front of us, but we are to take our position in the heavenlies in order to cut off Lucifer's supply.

Divine dissatisfaction is a quality we have sorely needed in Christian leaders. We have paid dearly for its absence. Here is where the real cost has been—in sustained revival!

We have had many revivals. Getting revival is not the hard part, it is keeping revival pure and effective. How soon revival leaders lose their hunger and their fight! They are so easily derailed into either emotional binges or the cooling influence of respectability.

After victory, there is so little of that hungry pursuit that demands balance and fire. That pursuit should be the heart of the revival.

Joash was a plain example of a person who

demonstrated lack of pursuit. We studied him in the letter on conation. Now look at how his inward satisfaction defeated him:

"And he said, 'Open the east window'; and he opened it. Then Elisha said, 'Shoot'; and he shot. And he said, 'The arrow of the Lord's deliverance and the arrow of deliverance from Syria; for you must strike the Syrians at Aphek till you have destroyed them'" [II Kings 13:17]. Here Joash is promised victory. But, he must beat the ground in pursuit of total destruction of the enemy: "Then he said, 'Take the arrows'; so he took them. And he said to the king of Israel, 'Strike the ground'; so he struck three times, and stopped. And the man of God was angry with him, and said, 'You should have struck five or six times; then you would have struck Syria till you had destroyed it! But now you will strike Syria only three times.'" [II kings 13:18-19].

Joash beat the Syrians three times, but he did not pursue them and cut off their threat. They later regrouped and returned to destroy.

Human nature has a vile propensity to grab a quick win and then be content. The Apostle Peter fought this weakness. Look at two examples:

Jesus was walking on the water. Peter had to try it! Jesus gave him permission. Peter started out, but soon began to sink. Jesus asked Peter why he doubted.

The reason for Peter's doubt was that fear and uncertainty convinced him that a good thing could not last! Out on the water, his fire for miracle power waned. He realized what he was doing, and it terrified him! He said to himself, "Okay. I've done it. That's enough."

Later in Peter's life, he would face this fear and become truly, divinely dissatisfied. He won this inner war at the Gate Beautiful.

Everyday Peter passed the lame man, and everyday he made sure he had money to give to him. The war for the man's healing had been fought and won, but God needed a pursuer. Peter's heart was filled with turmoil.

Jesus had told him he would die a martyr. This hung over Peter like a cloud. Peter knew well that his Master was persecuted for healing the sick. It was the prospect of persecution and death that froze Peter from going to the next level of power!

Not only that, but he had just seen the miracle harvest of Pentecost. Once again, his spirit said, "That's enough." But then the Holy Spirit touched him with a restless hunger for more. This fire within increased the pain of his compromise. The pain grew and grew until that wonderful day when the pain of staying average was far greater than his fear of danger. That morning, he refused to carry money to the temple because he was carrying something better.

He cast a mighty gaze on the paralyzed man and roared, "Silver and gold I do not have, but what I do have I give you: In the name of Jesus Christ of Nazareth, rise up and walk" [Acts 3:6].

All through my letters, I have told you about what the church and its warriors lack. I have tried to instruct you to leave the foolishness of religion and take up the life you were meant to have. I have told you to take up the armor, to be filled with the Spirit, and to possess all of the good gifts of God. Now, for once, I am saying that I want you to lack something, to be so devoid of it that you never recover from your need of it! You should always desperately desire greater victories.

I want you to never be satisfied.
I want you to be divinely dissatisfied!

—Martin

Comfort

Dear Warrior,

The story is told of a time when Satan conferred with his high command. The subject of the conference was the disturbing effectiveness of a single man of God and what should be done to stop him.

One demon stepped forward and suggested that a beautiful woman should be sent to seduce him and ruin him.

Satan waved off this idea by saying, "I know him. He would convert her. We would only be losing another soul."

The next demon proposed giving him great wealth so that he would be consumed by the love of money and weakened irreparably by opulent leisure.

Satan growled back, "That's an even worse idea because this man has no love of money and would put everything we give him into projects that would cost us even more souls."

Even after long reflection, they found no solution. Finally, a dark and wicked spirit presented itself before Satan.

"Master," it said, "I will go and discourage him." Satan's eyes widened and a wicked smile slowly stole across his face.

"Yes," he said in a low and deliberate murmur. "That's it exactly! Go and do it!"

Generals in all wars learn quickly about troop morale. A general must, at all costs, keep the killer frost of fear off of his men. Fear in a fighting force instantly ruins the best of training, plans, and opportunity. A general must also smite apathy and confusion as vigilantly as he would any physical invader. Hunger and fatigue are two other mortal enemies that a wise general will prevent at all costs.

Concerning troop morale, Von Clausewitz said, "One might say that the physical seemed little more than the wooden hilt while the morale factors are the precious metal, the real weapon, the finely honed blade."[40] If morale is the steel blade of war, then a great deal of effort must be placed into keeping it sharp. While troop morale is enhanced by courage, focus of purpose, physical nourishment, and rest, nothing compares to the morale-inducing power of the general himself.

Sun Tzu called the wise general "the respected one." He insisted that an effective commander must be a mystical, awe-inspiring figure to his men. He must, of necessity, possess strong virtues that inspire boldness in battle and, at the same time, dread and fear of his command. Sun Tzu said, "By command I mean the general's qualities of wisdom, sincerity, humanity, courage, and strictness: . . . These five are the virtues of the general. Hence the army refers to him as 'The Respected One' . . . If *wise*, a commander is able to recognize changing circumstances and to act expediently. If *sincere*, his men will have no doubt of the certainty of rewards and punishments. If *humane*, he loves mankind, sympathizes with others, and appreciates their industry and toil. If *courageous*, he gains victory by seizing opportunity without hesitation. If *strict*, his troops are disciplined because they are in awe of him and are afraid of punishment. . . . If a general is not courageous he will be unable to conquer doubts or to create great plans."[41]

The general who can conquer the fears and doubts of his men can conquer any outside enemy. Likewise, the general who convinces his men that he truly cares about them will win their undying loyalty.

Sun Tzu also said, "When one treats people with benevolence, justice, and righteousness, and reposes confidence in them, the army will be united in mind and all will be happy to serve their leaders."[42]

This union of soldier to his commander is the soul of morale. Von Clausewitz called this the "military spirit," when he said, "An army that maintains its cohesion under the most murderous fire; that cannot be shaken by imaginary fears and resists well-founded ones with all of its might; that, proud of its victories, will not lose the strength to obey orders and its respect and trust for its officers even in defeat; whose physical power like the muscles of an athlete, have been steeled by training in privation and effort; a force that regards such efforts as a means to victory rather than a curse on its cause; that is mindful of these duties and qualities by virtue of the single powerful idea of the honor of its arms —such an army is imbued with the true military spirit."[43]

But you, warrior, must also watch your morale. Your Commander-in-Chief longs to protect it. But let us call morale by its true name—*the comfort of the Holy Spirit.*

To understand this supernatural warrior-gift from God, we must begin by realizing that all the qualities that a soldier reveres in a mighty general are present in Christ but on a much more infinite scale. We are not merely cared for, we have been "bought with a price," and we are "loved with an everlasting love."

We must also fear the Lord: "The fear of the Lord is the beginning of wisdom; a good understanding have all those who do His commandments . . ." [Psalms 111:10]. His commands must be obeyed. The consequences of disobedience are as real for us in our daily life as they are to any soldier on a battlefield.

An absence of troop morale spells doom. Its spiritual equivalent is *discouragement.* Discouragement is a familiar word, and because it is, its danger is totally underrated. I know of no other condition that is more dangerous to a Christian warrior, and yet, it is handled with such minor concern. Discouragement is a virile attack on your spirit's immune system. It means to get to the core of your being and riddle you with its malignancy. You will feel powerless to pray! You will look at all your achievements, and they will feel meaningless and futile. You will look up the road of your future with a crushing emotion. You will feel that nothing you will ever do will make a difference.

Action against discouragement must be swift and complete. Do not be a foolish hero; admit you are in trouble. Do not test your limits against discouragement. Above all, and hear me in this, you must learn to embrace the comfort of the Holy Spirit. Just as a general regroups, fires up, and corrects his men to bring them back to battleworthiness, so Jesus has set in place a process to restore effective warfare: *the encouragement of the Holy Spirit.*

The Holy Spirit is comfort; He is called the Comforter. Just as an earthly general cannot deprive His soldiers of morale, Jesus promised, "I will not leave you comfortless . . . " [John 14:18 KJV].

Here is a chilling, but factual statement: In Christian war, the difference between conqueror and casualty will most likely be decided by a single habit: *the ability to go and submit to the work of the Holy Spirit and receive comfort in times of discouragement.* Here is how you develop this:

1. *Have an ear to hear the Holy Spirit.*
   "He that has an ear to hear, let him hear what the Holy Spirit says to the churches . . ." [Rev. 2:7a].

Go back with me to the letter about *communion* where I expose the voice of shame versus the Holy Spirit. Now is the time to employ what you have learned. The ability to hear and know the difference between shame and the Spirit's voice can only be developed by regular exercise.

2. *Let the Holy Spirit refresh your sense of being eternally bonded to God.*
"Who shall separate us from the love of Christ? Shall tribulation, or distress, or persecution, or famine, or nakedness, or peril, or sword?" [Romans 8:5].

You are loved unconditionally. The Holy Spirit will speak creative words to you, and those words will wipe out insecurity and restore an unfiltered vision of your connection to Christ.

3. *Ask for specific directions out of your storm of discouragement. Do not question those orders!*

Low troop morale almost cost David his life at Ziklag. He and his soldiers had returned from a battle to find their village burned to ashes and their wives and children stolen by Amalekite raiders.

"Now David was greatly distressed, for the people spoke of stoning him, because the soul of all the people was grieved, every man for his sons and his daughters. But David strengthened himself in the Lord his God" [I Samuel 30:6].

David wastes not one breath in accusation

against God. Instead, he asks for direction to get out of the crisis.

> "So David inquired of the Lord saying, 'Shall I pursue this troop? Shall I overtake them?' And He answered him, 'Pursue, for you shall surely overtake them and without fail recover all'" [I Samuel 30:8].

David received a word from God! It is emphatic, clear, and all encompassing. The crowning moment of your time of comfort in the Holy Spirit is this unmistakable voice of direction and promise of triumph.

4. Accept correction!

It is clear that we often permit the Enemy an opening to break our morale. We cannot deny this. The Holy Spirit will shine a light on your sin. He will point out the violations that allowed you to be mugged.

> "Behold, You desire truth in the inward parts, and in the hidden part You will make me to know wisdom" [Psalm 51:6].

The Holy Spirit will drive us back to scriptures that confirm our carnal mistakes and expose even our best-kept secret sins.

"For the word of God is living and powerful, and sharper than any two-edged
sword, piercing even to the division of soul
and spirit, and of joints and marrow, and
is a discerner of the thoughts and intents of
the heart" [Hebrews 4:12].

Children act like discipline is the end of the
world. But loving correction makes them feel secure afterwards. So it is, that when we willingly
accept correction, we also feel mighty strength
and a sense of relief.

"Now no chastening seems to be joyful for
the present, but painful; nevertheless,
afterward it yields the peaceable fruit of
righteousness to those who have been
trained by it" [Hebrews 12:11].

The Comforter is not only central to our
power gifts, miracles, attacks, and strategies,
but also for the overriding gift of comforting us
in our discouragement. He has assured us that
he will lavish us with everything needed for our
success in war.

Our General is an unending source of comfort. "Blessed be the God and Father of our Lord
Jesus Christ, the Father of mercies and God of
all comfort, who comforts us in all our tribulation, that we may be able to comfort those who

are in any trouble, with the comfort with which we ourselves are comforted by God" [II Corinthians 1:3-4]. Not only do we get a dose of renewed fight, we can impart it to the soldiers around us who are discouraged.

The commandments of God that we notice most are the ones that require self-denial and sacrifice. There are others, however, that we do not treat as commands. For example, to God, the commandment to "fear not" is every bit as strict as the injunction against adultery. Paul's demand that the Philippians ". . . rejoice in the Lord. For me to write the same things to you is not tedious, but for you it is safe" [Philippians 3:1].

In John 14, Jesus did not pat the disciples on the head and say, "There. There." He looked intently at them and ordered, "Peace I leave with you; not as the world gives do I give to you. Let not your heart be troubled, neither let it be afraid" [John 14:27].

*Willful neglect of your fighting
morale is a Biblical sin against God!*

—Martin

SECRET #12

Obedience

Dear Warrior,

Obedience is the only principle of war that has the same name in Heaven as on Earth. This is because obedience is the ultimate principle, not only in war but in everything else.

If this attribute is so obvious, then why call it a secret? The answer lies in the nature of a secret. A secret is information withheld, and the best secret is when it isn't even known that a secret exists.

Satan has hidden the true meaning of obedience in plain sight because he knew that this is the last place we would look for it! Do you recall when I told you that the most dangerous lie was saying that the Christian life is *like* a war? Do you remember that it is because a figurative view of war during a literal war is the ultimate disaster?

We pray symbolic prayers. We read the Bible metaphorically and don theatrical armor and all the while we are taking real hits from the Devil's live ammunition.

Satan's synthetic for obedience is a close cousin and an old acquaintance. But before I pull the mask off this villain, let me declare it evil and vile beyond description. Let me curse it with all my might and speak with holy rage against its cancerous influence. Let it occupy a place of such infamy and shame that its evilness can only be exceeded by two other miscreants— Satan and Man's fallen nature!

Obedience's evil twin is volunteerism. To volunteer presupposes choice. The volunteer is out of "the goodness of my own heart" doing a favor. During all the labors of a volunteer, there is nursed the idea that "I am free to stop and start at my leisure."

Let me make it clear that I am not dismissing those who offer their time and talent freely to the work of God. They are not my definition of a volunteer. They are under the command of Christ and attached by the Holy Spirit's orders to a Christian ministry!

Volunteers expect rewards. They can control schedules, quality of work, and can narcotically revel in their "willingness." They reanimate the mandatory acts of Christianity into exemplary acts of heroism!

Listen and be warned by the very words of Jesus for they prove that no one in God's army is
a volunteer! "You did not choose Me, but I chose
you . . ." [John 15:16].

What is the reason for my railing against the
volunteer? Because they come so close in action,
yet produce nothing. They emulate the acts that
should bring results and cause demons to turn
tail and run. But evil doesn't run; it cheers on
this fraud.

True obedience *shivers the timbers* of Hell!
True obedience jettisons devils and unleashes
power like nothing else can! The volunteer is under the influence, but the obedient one is under
the Authority.

So now, let us pull this weed out by the root!
What happened when you were born again?
You did nothing lofty or even heroic when you
accepted God's rescue mission. God and God
alone did the heroics.

How can we face the angels with a sanc-
timonious look knowing that our choice was
Christ or eternal flames? That was no choice!

When the cruelty of the Cross was done, God
issued a command. Be saved by Christ!

> "Truly, these times of ignorance God over-
> looked, but now commands all men every-
> where to repent, because He has appointed
> a day on which He will judge the world in

righteousness by the Man whom He has ordained. He has given assurance of this to
all by raising Him from the dead" [Acts
17:30-31].

God never asked for volunteers! We are not exemplary because we pray or witness. It is our
duty!

"And which of you, having a servant
plowing or tending sheep, will say to him
when he has come in from the field, 'Come
at once and sit down to eat'? But will he
not rather say to him, 'Prepare something
for my supper, and gird yourself and serve
me till I have eaten and drunk, and afterward you will eat and drink'? Does he
thank that servant because he did the
things that were commanded him? I think
not. So likewise you, when you have done
all those things which you are commanded, say, 'We are unprofitable servants. We have done what was our duty to
do.'" [Luke 17:7-10]

We are not outstanding because we stay moral.
It is the most basic act of the obedient Christian
soldier.

But why is the spirit of the volunteer so per-
vasive? *It is attractive to the flesh because it gets*

credit for its actions. This is offensive to God because its tap root is the same one from which springs the deception of salvation by works!

This do-gooder approach has saddled us with weak, self-centered, powerless, flex-time believers. They use up pastors. They are sporadic as they celebrate their consistency. They will not interrupt their lifestyle to serve God, yet they feel so committed. Never have people who have done so little boasted of so much! But if Satan ever lost his use of them, they could be defeated by a flick to the nose. For now, they remain an effective contraceptive to revival.

The soldier is obedient. There is no army without command. Sun Tzu recorded an incident that illusrated that there is no substitute for obedience: "When Wu Chu'i fought against Ch'in, there was an officer who before battle was joined was unable to control his ardor. He advanced and took a pair of heads and returned. Wu Ch'i ordered him beheaded. The Army Commissioner admonished him, saying: 'This is a talented officer; you should not behead him.' Wu Ch'i replied: 'I am confident he is an officer of talent, but he is disobedient.' Thereupon he beheaded him."[44]

Physical war changes so quickly that the soldier must respond to orders without hesitation. His entire identity in the army is drawn from his being under authority.

There are three vital elements to true obedience. They are so completely the same to soldier or Christian that I will dispense with any comparisons.

1. *Commands must be clear!*

Paul asked, "For if the trumpet makes an uncertain sound, who will prepare for battle?" [I Corinthians 14:8]. Clarity of orders causes uniformity of action. There is no hesitation or excuse for disobedience. Clear commands also reveal the true soldier. Disobedience to a clear and basic order proves the disloyalty of the soldier.

The Christian life must begin with a clear command to repent. To dissipate the clarity of the command to repent and believe the gospel is to essentially ask for volunteers. Clear commands reveal the Christian. It is a true test of our salvation. I John 2:3 says, "Now by this we know that we know Him, if we keep His commandments."

2. *Action must be immediate!*

"As Jesus passed on from there, He saw a man named Matthew sitting at the tax office. And He said to him, 'Follow Me.' So he arose and followed Him."

On the battlefield, commanders do not have

time to explain. Response to a command must be immediate! Sun Tzu said, "When confronted by the enemy, respond to changing circumstances and devise expedients. How can these be discussed beforehand?"[45] The enemy may have committed a blunder. The commander has precious little time to seize the opportunity. He must be able to order the army to change directions in an instant.

Von Clausewitz described the obedient army in this way, "With them, boldness acts like a coiled spring, ready at anytime to be released."[46]

The Jesus-soldier obeys immediately. He does not look for explanations. He "runs with the vision." There is something deeply wrong with the disciple who vacillates and takes up old ways that he was ordered to abandon! So much valuable time is lost by over-analyzing the voice of God!

3. Obedience must be exact!

The general is not looking for the soldier to improve upon his command. He wants what was ordered to be done. The warrior cannot see the overall purpose of his act or how it connects to the efforts of those who will come after. He trusts his commanding officer. He trusts the wisdom of those who drew up the plans. He cannot see how important his actions are. There is no time, nor would it serve the principle of security for a high command to disseminate classified information.

Above all, the true warrior does not judge the glamor of his mission. He does not test it to see if it is worthy of his talents. He is content that if he obeys, an overall effect will be created that will lead to decisive victory.

Today's Christian fails here! They want ego-enhancing projects for Christ, not obedience that would produce an overall God-given awakening. They chafe at commands that are not explained, rehashed, and defended. They even want to help design the strategy of God. But most of all, they want to be sure that their heroics are carrying their signature.

Look at this example in I Samuel 15. King Saul received clear orders, but he would not obey them accurately. The prophet Samuel rebuked him when he said, "Now the Lord sent you on a mission, and said, 'Go, and utterly destroy the sinners, the Amalekites, and fight against them until they are consumed.' Why then did you not obey the voice of the Lord? Why did you swoop down on the spoil, and do evil in the sight of the Lord?" [I Samuel 15:18-19].

King Saul responded to Samuel and said, "But I have obeyed the voice of the Lord, and gone on the misson on which the Lord sent me, and brought back Agag king of Amalek; I have ut-

terly destroyed the Amalekites" [I Samuel 15:20].
He had altered the commandment, supposing
that he was improving it!

Samuel will not let volunteerism off the hook.
He exposed it, and all its ugly tentacles. "So
Samuel said: 'Has the Lord as great delight in
burnt offerings and sacrifices as in obeying the
voice of the Lord? Behold, to obey is better than
sacrifice, and to heed than the fat of rams. For
rebellion is as the sin of witchcraft, and stub-
bornness is as iniquity and idolatry. Because you
have rejected the word of the Lord, He also
has rejected you from being king'" [I Samuel 15:
22-23].

Here is not only the summation of this secret,
but of all *the twelve.* Lucifer has plied his lying
spirits long and hard to prevent pure and true
obedience. Churches are filled with wheat and
tares so that the power of the obedient cannot be
revealed.

The gates of Hell quake on their hinges at the
prospect of what you may do now. It is enough
for me that I know that soon after I have finished writing this manuscript, I will go to my re-
ward. No one in my family knows this, but the
Lord stood by me and gently let me know.

How can I impress upon you the urgency of
both the hour you live in and the indispensable
qualities of these *twelve secrets*? I will not live
to see that great global damage you will exact on

Satan, but I have decided to rejoice in it with all my might!

It is so strangely wonderful to say, "I love you," whoever you are, and that the love of God is what strengthened me against the immeasurable onslaught of Lucifer so that I could finish this mysterious treatise.

Even though these truths are as close to me as my next breath, they sometimes seem inexplicable. One thing has become clear . . . God has helped me build a bridge for you. It is up to you to cross it. Do I believe you will? You know I do! You see, you have been ruined just like me. There is not much about *this side* that dazzles once you've tasted glory and have felt the inner fire.

Love, Martin

EPILOGUE

12 Years Later

All is not well in Satan's Lair. Two especially disconcerted elite devils are huddled in a secluded part of the dark region. They are greatly agitated and are growling something back and forth to each other, but are trying to keep from being heard.

"I'm not going to tell him!" demanded the first.

"Yes, you are. I had to tell him the last time!" replied the other.

Suddenly, the entire region begins to quake and a deep rolling thunder dislodges boulders. They dash for cover in a nearby cave.

"Every year we go through this, but this year it is so much worse," said the first.

"I don't care. It is your turn, and that is it!" said the second.

"Can you even imagine what he is going to do to me?" asked the first. "We have never stopped

183

paying for letting that spy in here twelve years ago."

Suddenly, a meek voice in the back of the cave spoke up. "Excuse me, sirs, but what spy? And what bad news?"

The eavesdropping devil was of low rank and had darted into the cave just before them. This was a tense moment. Officers of Lucifer were under strict orders not to divulge anything about the spy affair.

Perhaps it was panic, or maybe arrogance, but the first senior devil began to explain, "Our security was breached twelve years ago."

The second officer screamed, "Stop! You must maintain the code of secrecy! Do you realize what the Master will do to you?"

The first officer shot back, "Do *you* realize what he is going to do to me once I give him this terrible news?"

Now, turning to the common demon, he continued. "That's right. We were invaded. An intruder heard our most sensitive secrets and he escaped. He actually materialized right in front of the Master and threatened us all! Not only that, the trespasser said he was going to find *the twelve*."

These words did not just shock the worker devil, they put him in a stupor. This basic demon could no more grasp what the officer meant by *the twelve* than a toddler could do calculus.

This whole time the other officer kept shouting at his cohort to shut up!

But nothing, not the blank look of the demon nor the rebuke of his partner, could stop this now hysterical leader from spilling everything.

"Now," he said, "what was that intruder's name? Come on, old buddy, you remember. . ."

The second officer, now resigned to the inevitable, blurted out, "Daniel!"

"Oh, yes," said the first devil sarcastically. "*Daniel*. I hated that name before I ever heard of *this* guy! Here we were doing everything in our power to keep people from finding this miserable document. And how was it discovered? Daniel found out about it from us! Isn't that rich? From us!" Then this frenzied ghoul let out a loud, long, and dreadful laugh of despair.

"Finally," he continued, "Daniel goes back to where he came from, and *What do you know?* He finds *the twelve*. And, of course, he prays and prays and prays. So then, bingo! He starts a movement. Not just any movement. Not this guy. He has to go crazy! And get this, he calls his movement *Matthew 24:14*. The group took off like a hurricane. Now they are everywhere, and worst of all, they are mainly students! All year long they do us harm. It is at this same time every year that they really do damage!"

"Why this time of year?" asked the hapless common demon.

"Because, Sulfer Breath, every year Daniel

has a huge deal on the anniversary of the day he found *the twelve*! And, can you guess which day that is?"

"Ahhh . . . no," said the worker devil.

"October 31st! Isn't that perfect!" bellowed the first officer.

With that, he reached over and grabbed the low-ranking spirit by the neck.

"So, do you know what I have to do tonight? I have the distinct honor of giving Lucifer the worst news he has had in years. And when he hears it, he is going to grab me and fling me with such force that I will more than likely be embedded in granite for a long, long time!

"I've got to tell the Master that Daniel is going to fill football stadiums by the hundreds, all on the same night, and then hook them all together by satellite! We are talking about *millions* of youth in attendance!"

Suddenly, the evil regions began to quake again, even more violently.

"What was that?" asked the demon.

"That," said the officer, "is the prayers of the *Matthew 24:14* movement. And that's nothing compared to what is coming—especially to me —since my buddy here *insists* that I make the announcement."

"You mean about the gatherings," asked the spirit.

"No. Satan already knows all about that. It is even worse news," said the senior devil.

Once again, a quake came, only this time it covered them in rubble. After they dug out, the worker demon had to ask, "What is your bad news, sir?"

At that moment, Satan's signal rang out for all of his elite to gather. No officer dared hesitate.

As they flew off, the officer yelled back at the demon, "The bad news is that they are announcing tonight that they are going international! They are going to go into *all* the world!"

And, with this, the flying demon laughed loudly and hideously, and could be heard until he flew out of sight.

ENDNOTES

1. Tzu, Sun. *The Art of War*. Ed. by Samuel B. Griffith. London: Oxford University Press, 1963: p. 64.
2. *Ibid*. p. 71.
3. Mathews, R. Arthur. *Born for Battle*. New York: Banta Company, 1978: p. 67.
4. Tzu, p. 65.
5. Jomini, Baron Antoine Henri (1779-1869). General who served under Napoleon. One of the founders of modern military thought.
6. Tzu, p. 41.
7. Wilson, Jim. *Principles of War*. Annapolis: Christian Books, 1964: pp. 26-27.
8. Tzu, p. 69.
9. *Ibid*. p. 69.
10. *Ibid*. p. 41.
11. *Ibid*. p. 65.
12. *Ibid*. p. 101.
13. *Ibid*. p. 98.
14. *Ibid*. p. 106.
15. Mathews, p. 52.
16. Wilson, p. 46.
17. Tzu, p. 85.
18. *Ibid*. p. 42.
19. *Ibid*. p. 42.
20. *Ibid*. p. 85.

21. *Ibid.* p. 87.
22. *Ibid.* p. 114.
23. Seldes, George. *The Great Quotations.* New York: Carol Publishing Group, 1993: p. 67.
24. Howard, Michael and Paret, Peter, Eds. *On War.* New York: Everyman's Library, 1993: p. 233. General Carl Von Clausewitz (1780-1831) served under Napoleon. He is considered a great military historian and intellectual of the highest degree.
25. *Ibid.* p. 233.
26. Tzu, p. 108.
27. *Ibid.* p. 92.
28. Howard and Paret, p. 233.
29. Tzu, pp. 135-136.
30. *Ibid.* p. 138.
31. Howard and Paret, p. 412.
32. Tzu, p. 65.
33. Mathews, p. 117.
34. Howard and Paret, p. 250.
35. Mathews, p. 55.
36. Howard and Paret, p. 313.
37. *Ibid.* p. 312.
38. *Ibid.* p. 319.
39. Tzu, p. 137.
40. Howard and Paret, p. 217.
41. Tzu, p. 65.
42. Tzu, p. 66.
43. Howard and Paret, p. 220.
44. Tzu, p. 107.
45. *Ibid.* p. 70.
46. Howard and Paret, p. 223.

Other Books by Mario Murillo

Critical Mass
Embedded in II Chronicles 7:14 are instructions to follow in order to remove Satan's vile talons from the throat of our nation. *Critical Mass* is about the yearning that many Christians have to see a new act of God. It is a strategy for revival in our land!

Fresh Fire
This book is a guide to fresh baptisms in the Holy Spirit. There await us new drenchings of holy power—power that will more than match the flood of evil in this final moment of mankind. This book is not one more "bless-me-quick ditty." It is a book for those who want to thrive spiritually amid the insanity of these last days.

Fresh Impact
Here is a message of fire! It will stir your mind and heart and will help you understand that when *fresh fire* falls on you, it inflames you to go and do unimaginable exploits—and their effects. This book is one that prepares us for a mighty move of the Holy Spirit which is promised by Almighty God!